HEAL'S POSTERS

# Advertising
# Modernism

Ruth Artmonsky & Stella Harpley

Published by:
Artmonsky Arts
Flat 1, 27 Henrietta Street
London WC2E 8NA
artmonskyruth@gmail.com
Tel. 020 7240 8774

Text © Ruth Artmonsky 2020

ISBN 978-0-9935878-9-4

Designed by:
David Preston Studio
www.davidprestonstudio.com

Printed in England by:
Northend Creative Print Solutions
www.northend.co.uk

As usual, my thanks go to my designers David and Tamsin at David Preston Studio for their innovation and wit.

| Contents | | |
|---|---|---|
| | Foreword | 7 |
| | Introduction | 9 |
| | The 'Modernist' Poster | 13 |
| | Heal's Men (and one woman) | 19 |
| | Heal's Shop | 25 |
| | Heal's Advertising | 33 |
| | Heal's Artists and their Posters | 45 |
| | Art Exhibition Posters | 59 |
| | Furniture Posters | 71 |
| | Etcetera | 93 |
| | Epilogue | 115 |
| | Bibliography | 117 |
| | Appendix | 118 |

# Foreword

Heal's seems to have always been part of my life, from when, on leaving university and settling in London, I became a young newly-wed yearning for my own home but totally impecunious. On a Saturday morning we would visit Heal's, using it as a learning resource, a museum of good design, daydreaming of what we would buy when we could afford to. At first we managed to save for modest purchases – some Ernest Race 'Antelope' dining chairs, some Lucienne Day fabric, 'Rig', for curtaining – and, eventually, for our first house, a Danish teak wardrobe. Fast forward some sixty years, now living in a loft in Covent Garden, I besport a large piece of Lucienne Day's 'Calyx' over my Heal's bed and a swathe of 'Sequoia' over my Heal's chairs.

    An idle moment on Google recently informed me of an antique dealer selling three vintage Heal's posters. Within a month, fuelled by nostalgia, I had acquired eight. Lying in bed each night and awakening each morning, staring at these, now on my bedroom wall, I pondered as to why in research for my books on advertising

Opposite page: View of Heal's sale poster on the platform at Tottenham Court Road Central line station, 1974.

Heal's posters on show at Heal's central London shop, Tottenham Court Road.

I had so rarely come across references to the fact that Heal's had produced such interesting posters; and not too long afterwards the possibility of a book came to mind.

Imagine my chagrin and frustration when I was given Oliver Heal's splendid book on his grandfather, Sir Ambrose Heal, so thoroughly researched, not a stone left unturned, not a byway unexplored, yet eminently readable and wonderfully illustrated. Stella, my co-author, pointed out that we had already done some relevant research in preparation for two books – *Showing Off* on London store advertising, and *Tuppence Plain, Penny Coloured* on the advertising of the furniture trade, and that, in any case, Oliver's focus was on Sir Ambrose and his furniture designing and that 'posters' were only touched upon on three out of the three hundred pages of the book. Bolstered by this and energised by nostalgia, we decided, to try to restore the reputation of Heal's posters as fine examples of twentieth century graphics, publicising the modernism of one of London's major furniture retailers.

# Introduction

The Victoria & Albert Museum hold the National Collection of posters – some ten thousand, both home-grown and foreign. And it was the V&A that validated the poster as an art form, and thereby upped the status of the poster artist, when it mounted the first large scale exhibition of posters in 1931. From 1978 to 1999 some half dozen gifts and one batch purchase brought the archives of Heal's to Blythe Road, the V&A archives of rt and design. Amongst Heal's 4700 files were some two hundred posters. Images of some of the best-preserved ones can be seen on the museum's website and viewed in its study centre; otherwise the cache is relatively untapped.

    One might ask why the neglect, when myriads of articles and books have been written about posters – posters hyping petrol and oil, and travelling by rail, road and air, and from the government informing and persuading us? In all this commentating on posters there is barely a mention of posters for selling furniture and furnishings as a genre, or of Heal's posters in particular.

The Heal's bulding, 1854.

The Heal's building, 1916.

Why then, if others have not given furniture posters a thought should a relatively small neglected hoard merit a book? Well firstly just for that reason – they are a rarity. The furniture trade has advertised its wares in press advertisements and features in magazines since the middle of the nineteenth century, but rarely has it been thought profitable to expend budgets on posters. Only as large a firm as The Times Furnishing Company, which prior to WWII had some thirty branches in London and some half dozen beyond, could afford and find it worthwhile to resort to the hoardings to publicise its name and its locations. When it came to a company the size of Heal's, located for most of its history on one site, making use of posters would have been exceptional.

But there are reasons beyond mere rarity to now laud Heal's posters, for they tell tales – of the history of twentieth century furniture design, of the ups and downs of the furniture trade, of the development of graphics as a profession – as well as a potted history of a particular enterprise, a company on a mission, pioneering its own brand of British modernism.

In appreciating Heal's posters they need to be seen against the background of the men and the company who commissioned them, and the general development of the poster in the twentieth century.

# The 'Modernist' Poster

The twentieth century saw the growth and decline of the poster. Although poster historians are tempted to trace the poster back to trade signs on the walls of Pompeii and the like, the poster, as we know it today, emerges in the Victorian era, its development hand-in-glove with the increasing technical sophistication of the printing process.

Margaret Timmers, the notable poster historian, in *The Power of the Poster*, provides a brutally pared down definition of what a poster is:

> ...a product of communication between an active force and a reactive one. Its originator... has a message to sell; the recipient, its target, must be persuaded to buy the message. The interchange takes place in public.

Susan Sontag, perhaps a less enthusiastic fan, spells out possible 'motivations' within the 'force', both positive and negative – to seduce,

Poster by Joost Schmidt for the first Bauhaus exhibition in 1923. Merging image and copy, the design shows the School's experimental style.

to exhort, to sell, to educate, to convince, to appeal. To these, other commentators would add that a poster should be attached to a wall, not on it; and that it should be multiple, there should be more than one copy.

Early British posters merely consisted of supposedly attractive pictures, not infrequently supplied by Royal Academicians, with texts attached to the bottom. The French claim to have had the first full-time professional poster designer – Jules Cheret – with his buxom long-tressed girls, often having little relevance to the product being hyped.. And certainly it was customary, in Britain, for jobbing printers to hold stocks of images that they would proffer for selling soaps or cars or patriotism, it did not matter which – the name of the organisation sending the message to be placed beneath the picture.

But then came 'modernism', wafting over from the Continent. Dr David Preston, of University of the Arts London, suggests that the word 'reductive' neatly and most economically encapsulates what happened to graphics, and, in this instance, posters, as a result. All elements of image and text were reduced, colours became primary and powerful rather than subtle, the idea to be carried became distilled, abstract or symbolic. Yet 'modernism' demanded that in spite of reduction, design should be dynamic – the 'force' of Timmer's definition.

With the experimental graphics of the likes of Moholy-Nagy and Herbert Bayer at the Bauhaus, type lost its curls and whirls, its unnecessary decoration, and became clean-cut and mechanistic; and

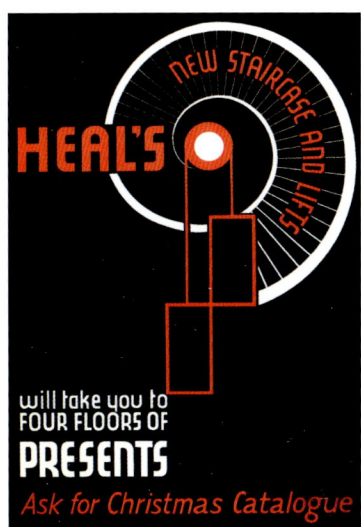

Heal's poster from 1933 echoing the colour, typography and layouts of Bauhaus 'modernism'. Designer uncredited.

type became integral to the overall design – not merely horizontal, but vertical, diagonal and curved; not below the image but embedded in it; whilst the image, itself, became increasingly abstract and geometric.

In London, Frank Pick, of the Underground, was raising awareness of the importance of type in communication with his commissioning of Edward Johnston, resulting in the introduction of simple block lettering without serifs. Although Johnston's alphabet was primarily for signage on underground stations and at bus stops, it set a standard that was soon to infect public lettering in general, and posters in particular. And it was Pick who 'discovered' Edward McKnight Kauffer, who was to bring a new language, a 'modernism' to poster design, that was to be a model for other designers in Britain. McKnight Kauffer stated his case:

> ...we live in a scientific age of T-squares and compasses.
> The attention, therefore, is attracted by the geometric and
> geometric design is retained longer in the memory than
> pure pictorial.

The French 'modernist' poster designers, Paul Colin and Cassandre, over-lapped with McKnight Kauffer, who worked in Britain up to WWII. In the wake of Kauffer came Tom Purvis and Austin Cooper; and then the wave of emigres in the mid-1930s, including Hans Schleger, F.H.K. Henrion and Abram Games, the true integrators of text and image.

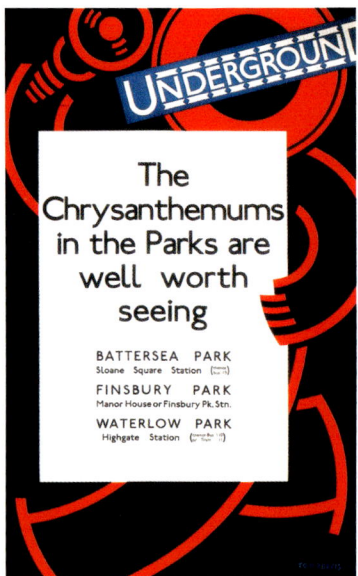

Poster by Tom Purvis for London Transort breaking down image and text, 1932.

Frank Pick, as patron of poster designers, was a role model for such other pioneers as Stephen Tallents at the Empire Marketing Board and the Post Office, Jack Beddington at Shell, and William Teasdale of the London Northern & Eastern Railways (LNER). Pick, who was once described as 'the nearest approach to Lorenzo the Magnificent that a modern democracy could achieve', served as a model for Ambrose Heal, a fellow member of the progressive Design & Industries Association; not only as a model, for it was Pick who provided the wall space on the underground for Heal's posters, from whom Heal borrowed some of his poster artists, and whose poster printer, Dangerfield, Heal's adopted for its own.

Although Ambrose, with his relatively small enterprise to advertise, can in no way be placed with the celestial throng listed above, he was someone who took great care with his advertising, took full responsibility for it, and had the knowledge and enthusiasm for graphic design to ensure interesting results. Ambrose, although a writer on a number of topics, actually penned little about his company's advertising policy or its posters, although he did once attempt to establish what he considered the characteristics of a 'good' poster:

> It must be arresting, attractive and apposite, it must compel attention either by its humour or by the suggestion of a pleasant idea; it must definitely suggest the goods and link them up with the idea.

1950s poster by Feeney for Heal's displaying a reductive, modernistic style and simple use of colour.

This is altogether more gentlemanly than Timmers with her 'forcefulness'; and the suggestion of humour is curious, in that furniture advertising, either in the press or by posters, rarely made use of humour, and Ambrose, himself, was not characterised for his jollity. It was not until the 1960s that Heal's produced even a smirk into its posters, with Feeney's rickety chair and wobbly glasses.

Heal's posters had a touch of modernism from the start, although never quite matching up to the radicalism of Kauffer's early posters for exhibitions of the London Group at Heal's Mansard Gallery. Nevertheless, Heal's met most of the criteria of modernism in its posters through to the 1970s, whether done by some au courant commercial artist or by some relatively unknown one.

That the poster, always a minor element in publicity compared to press advertisements, was to decline, was not merely because of the deskilling of graphic design by the adoption of photography, and, towards the end of the century, by the arrival of the computer, but by the beginning of commercial radio and then, commercial television – and finally internet – if you can get to people in their own homes, hit them personally, then why resort to the expense of hoardings.

# HEAL'S MEN (and one woman)

Ambrose Heal was the great grandson of the firm's founder, John Harris Heal; and he, in turn, would be followed by his two sons, Anthony and Christopher and his grandson, Oliver – a family that ran the business for some one hundred and seventy years, from 1810 to 1983. Oliver wrote of his grandfather:

> It was his defining hand that ultimately ordered and designed everything from the selection of the merchandising, the advertising and the graphics, to the layout and rebuilding of the shop.
>
> (Not forgetting that he also designed a good deal of the firm's furniture, through to the early 1930s)

Ambrose was a complex personality – as a youth more often to be seen on the playing field than in art or woodwork classes, yet to mature into a noted furniture designer; an introvert, largely shunning the

Opposite page: Sir Ambrose Heal, Heal's Chairman from 1913–1953. Photography by Walter Benington, for Elliott & Fry, 1930s.

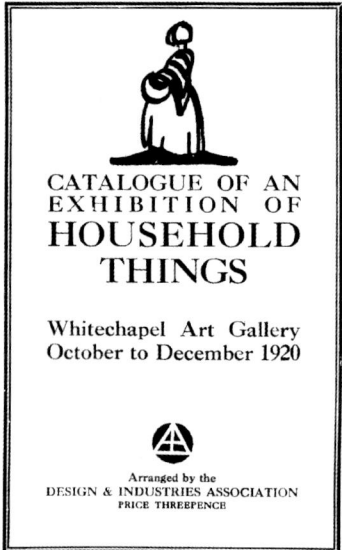

Exhibition catalogue for the Design & Industries Association which Ambrose Heal helped to found, 1920. Heal's supplied much of the merchandise on show at the exhibition.

limelight, described as 'withdrawn and unsociable', yet a remarkable networker when it counted; a man with his heart in the past, inspired by the Arts & Crafts movement, researching historical aspects of London trades, yet with a business head that was focused not only on the contemporary but on the future, alert to what was going on in this country and abroad and ready to risk all on 'modernism'. Even Ambrose's appearance was atypical for his trade – fine tweeds, exquisite hand-made shirts, eighteenth century folding glasses. looking like 'a poet in a black felt hat'.

A reference in the *Journal of the Royal Society of Arts* in 1929 described where he stood on 'modernism':

> Ambrose Heal is a modern rather in the way Bernard Shaw is a modern. He is direct and earnest and never more conservative than when he is being emancipated.

Ambrose was an Arts & Crafts man who understood and accepted the role of machinery in furniture manufacturing, and it was this that led him, and his cousin Cecil Brewer, to help found the Design & Industry Association (DIA) in 1915, and made him a modernist. He readily took up the cause of the Association – 'to encourage a more intelligent demand amongst the public for what is best and soundest in design'. Heal's, under Ambrose, became more than a shop selling furniture and furnishings, it grew to be a role model and an educator. A 1935 poster, by Norman Weaver, 'Art in Industry at Heal's', itself

Christopher Heal, 1953. Ambrose's youngest son Christopher became Heal's design director in 1952, with his brother, Anthony, appointed chairman soon after.

a good example of modernist graphics, exemplifies Ambrose's values and his careful oversight of Heal's publicity. Ambrose, although perhaps a shade reluctant to plunge headfirst into radical European modernism, nevertheless began to build a reputation as a modernist to the extent that Nicolas Pevsner felt he should be included in his *Pioneers of the Modern Movement*; and his obituarist, Robert Harling, wrote of him:

> ...he broke out of the Victorian straightjacket and brought some kind of sanity into British furniture design.

Ambrose was to remain something of an 'eminence gris' at Heal's even after he had retired from most of its operational responsibilities. Nevertheless he had the commercial sense and foresight to hand over to his sons the running of the business by the mid-1930s. Noel Carrington, the design commentator and editor, reported a conversation with Ambrose at about that time in which he said:

> You know, of course, that I was brought up on the bench. But the young men must have their head.

The 'young men' were his sons, Anthony (b. 1907) and Christopher (b. 1911). Anthony, a graduate of Grenoble University, joined the firm in 1929, having had an 'apprenticeship' with Gordon Russell. He was to work on the commercial and managerial side of the business,

Anthony Heal who served as chairman from 1952 to 1981.

although there is an example of some lighting he designed that was manufactured by the General Electric Company and shown with Heal's other products in the 1935 exhibition at Burlington House, 'British Art in Industry'. Initially Anthony took over responsibility for advertising, but by 1936 he was a director and, from 1953, on Ambrose's death he became, the firm's Chairman. Although not directly involved in design he was a strong promoter of modernism, was active in the various furniture trade associations and became a member of the Government's new Council of Industrial Design from 1959 to 1967. His enthusiasm and active support for good design earned him the Royal Society of Arts Bi-centenary medal for his influence in promoting art and design in British industry. That Anthony was heir to much of his father's values is exemplified in a quote of Anthony addressing a group of the shop's new buyers and managers:

> The setting and maintenance of high standards of design and quality is not easy. It calls for imagination, conviction and a good deal of guts... you must have 'concern' in the Quaker sense of the word; a sense of mission and the conviction of a just cause.

Ambrose's younger son, Christopher, joined the firm in 1934, having read architecture and economics at Cambridge and then studied textiles and furniture design at Central School of Art &

Prudence Maufe, 1930.

Design. He was to become a key furniture designer for the shop and Director of its Design Studio from 1952 to 1975. Christopher's designs were continuously on sale in the shop, on show at exhibitions, and were featured in the press. Lesley Jackson in her book on post-war British furniture design describes him as a 'pragmatic idealist' and that could well be a description of all three Heal's men – men with a mission but well aware of the realities of commercial life.

C. Edwards, in a thesis on the history of Tottenham Court Road, describes Heal's as 'a beacon of tasteful contemporary design', 'tasteful', with its slightly snide innuendo, was a word not usually applied to Heal's or to Heal's men. But one woman was described as Heal's arbiter of 'good taste and design' and that was Prudence Maufe, Ambrose's amour, who had joined Heal's around 1915 as 'adviser on interior decoration'. Prudence became key to what went on in the top floor of the shop – for its 'show flat' she acted as 'ensembler', selecting furniture and furnishings for exhibition rooms, whilst keeping an eye on what was to go on in its Mansard Gallery. That she rose to be Heal's first woman director in 1939 and contributed to the start-up of Heal's Fabrics after the war, was entirely due to her considerable talents and strong personality. In that she was a modernist in despising the craftiness of 'hollow hearts in wooden chairs and bedsteads' that had crept into Heal's furniture early in the century, would have been a further influence, along with that of his sons, in keeping Ambrose's eye on both the contemporary and the future.

# Heal's Shop

Now, two decades into the twentieth century Tottenham Court Road is still a magnet for furniture shops, which cluster together as tailors did in Savile Row or art galleries in Cork Street. For some two hundred years the road and abutting streets have been awash with furniture makers and dealers, originally small specialist workshops with families and apprentices living alongside, then evolving into multistoried emporia selling everything needed in a home from pots and pans to complete suites of furniture. Heal's had as its neighbours Shoolbred, Maples, Wolfe & Hollander, with Oetzman's just beyond on Hampstead Road and Waring & Gillows and the Times Furnishing Co. on New Oxford Street. Of all these only Heal's remains, its imposing building standing out from the myriad of small furniture shops along the road seeming to be continuously changing hands.

Heal's had started out as a workshop manufacturing mattresses in Rathbone Place, a small parallel road. With the business burgeoning it initially moved to 203 Tottenham Court Road before settling on the site that was to become 196 – the number resplendent

below Heal's name on all its early posters. By the 1850s Heal's was showing itself off in a monstrous Italianate building designed by one J. Morant Lockyer, which, in its turn, was to have a rebuild by Ambrose's cousin Cecil Brewer in 1917. Each change to the building served as an opportunity to publicise the firm and the modernity it stood for. Brewer's design with its frontage of Portland stone and its concave ground floor windows, made a clear statement that here was a furniture shop with a difference – 'modernism' had arrived on Tottenham Court Road.

Brewer's development made room for a show flat on the top floor along with an exhibition space, aptly named the Mansard Gallery; whilst his spiral staircase is still, today, on the 'visitors to London' list of 'must sees'. The Mansard Gallery was to feature some

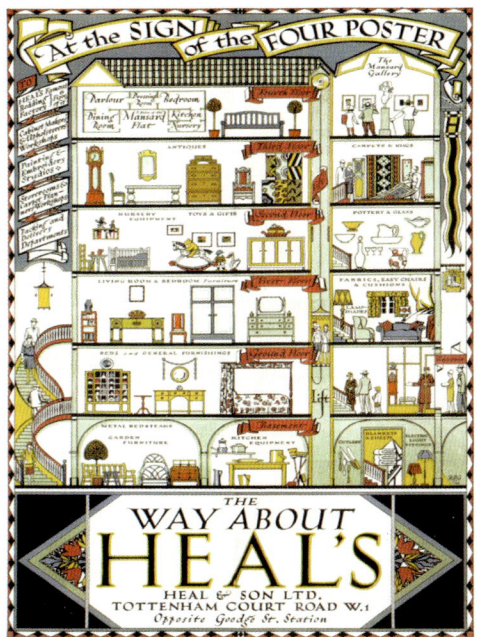

Opposite page: A hoarding designed for Heal's, 1915. Planned by R.P. Gossop, with panels designed and painted by Minnie McLeish and lettering by Percy J. Smith.

Above: R.P. Gossop's splendid poster displaying the range of Heal's merchandise, 1928.

Right: Gossop's poster displayed on a safety curtain at the Lyric Theatre, London, undated.

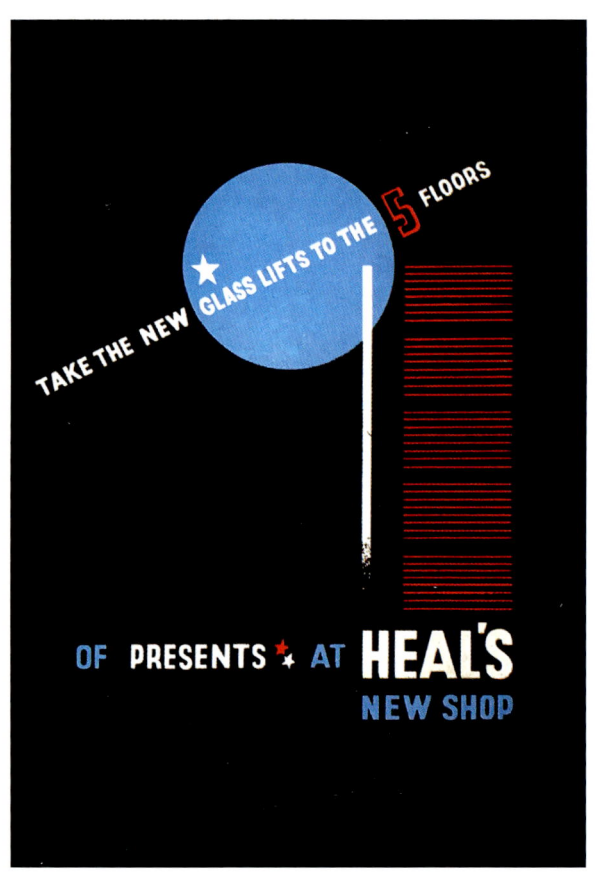

Opposite page, left: Rodney Hooper's poster for Heal's extension, 1937.

Opposite page, right: Unsigned Kauffer-esque leaflet from 1937 publicising five floors of presents.

Above: Charles Feeney's 1950s poster for Heal's shop extension.

of the most avant garde art exhibitions in the early 1920s and some of the most modernist furniture and furnishings exhibitions, through to the post-war years. When critics suggested that the Gallery was just an advertising ploy Heal's responded in an advertisement along the lines 'so what!' – in that you can tell the character of a shop by its advertising and they were proud of it. The Mansard Gallery, although never a commercial success, was, in fact, a successful 'ploy' as it attracted the great and the good of the professional cultured classes to the shop. A 1920 advertisement in *Colour* included a recommendation:

> I know of no other modern business building in London which can compare with Heal's new shop in its classic simplicity, its characteristic yet unadorned modernity.

Reginald Gossop's 1928 poster gave a detailed picture of how the departments were laid out in Brewer's building, with visitors reaching the top floor to view the Mansard flat and Gallery. The poster sends the message that Heal's is not just about beds and bedding but can now furnish a whole home (and garden). And again, when Edward Maufe designed the shop's extension on its south side in 1937 (his grand multistoried window possibly inspired by his recent designs for Guildford Cathedral), there was to be much press coverage, particularly as Frank Pick, the modernist of the underground, was invited to open it declaring that here was:

Opposite page, left: Cover of a 4-page handbill sent to customers publicising the benefits of 'Heal's New Shop', c.1917.

Opposite page, right: Poster design by Helen Senior produced after Heal's was bought by the Storehouse group, 1984.

…a school of taste for a variety of pockets, rising new born in great splendour.

Rodney Hooper's poster, of 1937, announcing the 'new shop', although including the then graphically fashionable dismembered hand, is not a particularly strong example of contemporary graphics but that may well have been because Hooper was a furniture designer rather than a graphic artist – rather a regressive image compared to the 1933 poster announcing new lifts which had been altogether more in the style of McKnight Kauffer.

This tendency for Heal's to provide a poster for each building re-jigging extended into the post-war years with Charles Feeney's 'Heal's Extends' for the Herbert Robinson 1962 extension of the north-west corner. Feeney returned to the 'fourposter' of Heal's early advertising but gave it a contemporary twist. Conran was to copy the idea with a 1984 poster by Helen Senior showing the Habitat/Mothercare invasion of the same corner.

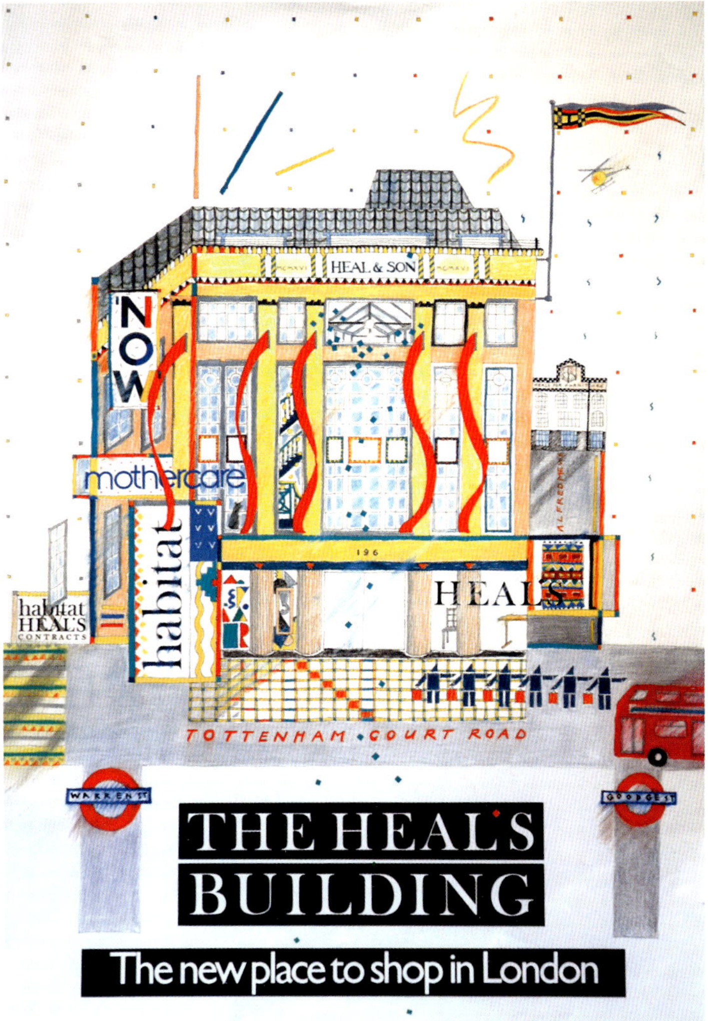

### a new approach to sitting down

The head-over-Heal's feeling is confusing me.  Here are all these wonderful new chairs, and I don't know whether to sit in them now or rush them home in a taxi. There's always something going on at Heal's; always something to see. Six floors full of the world's best in home-making design. Go right round Europe, you won't find a shop with so many beautiful things for your home, so much practical knowledge of fine design. Heal's in Tottenham Court Road is Europe's most exciting furniture shop. **For that can't-wait-to-get-it-home feeling...** HEAL'S

# Heal's Advertising

In appreciating the contribution that Heal's posters made to Heal's publicity they need to be seen in the context of Heal's overall advertising policy, along with its press advertisements, catalogues and exhibition stands. Oftimes the same images would be used for posters and press advertisements and occasionally one might make a playful reference to another as with a press advertisement showing a room with a Feeney poster on the wall. To get a true perspective it is necessary also to consider Heal's budgeting, as its allocation for posters would have been within a very small overall advertising budget compared, say, to that of The Times Furnishing Company. In the 1930s Heal's would have had annually perhaps about £4500 for total advertising and publicity whilst Times Furnishing Company had a budget of around £15,000 for posters alone.

    Heal's had been an early convert to the power of advertising when, for nearly thirty years, it had placed its advertisements in the magazines in which Dickens published his novels in instalments. By the mid-nineteenth century Heal's was advertising in such nationals as *The*

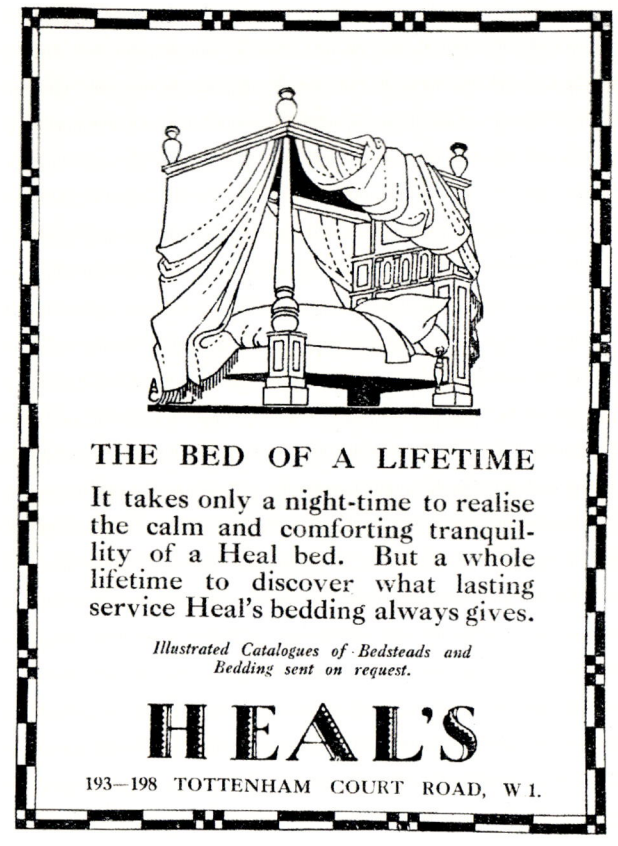

### THE BED OF A LIFETIME

It takes only a night-time to realise the calm and comforting tranquillity of a Heal bed. But a whole lifetime to discover what lasting service Heal's bedding always gives.

*Illustrated Catalogues of Bedsteads and Bedding sent on request.*

## HEAL'S
193—198 TOTTENHAM COURT ROAD, W.1.

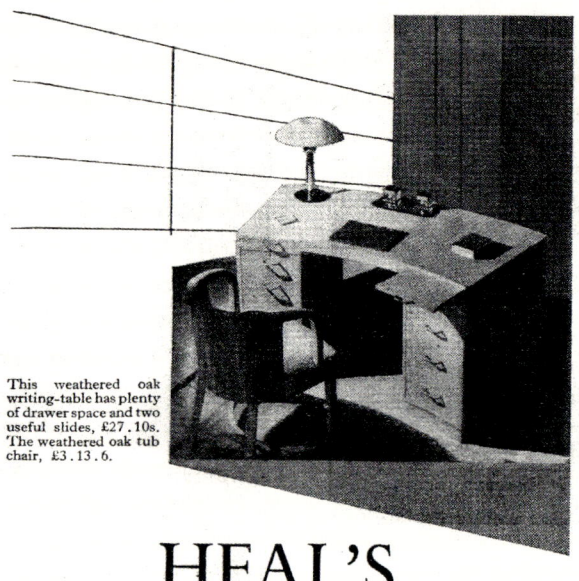

This weathered oak writing-table has plenty of drawer space and two useful slides, £27.10s. The weathered oak tub chair, £3.13.6.

## HEAL'S

*Where lovely things cost less than you expect*

HEAL & SON LTD · 196 TOTTENHAM COURT ROAD · W1

Opposite page, left: Typical press advertisement released under Ambrose Heal's direction, 1930.

Opposite page, right: An example of Heal's press advertisements after Anthony Heal took over responsibility for the company advertising, 1938.

Above: Two typical poster advertisements for the The Times Furnishing Company, 1938.

*Times, The Spectator, The Illustrated London News* and *Punch*. As Ambrose was to be an innovator in what his firm manufactured and sold, he was to have an immediate affect on its advertising when he was given responsibility for it in 1900. In what, in hindsight, can be seen as an early example of branding, Heal's press adverts became immediately recognisable on a page, with their checked borders and image of a four poster bed along with the tag 'At the Sign of the Four Poster'. These were meticulously designed in both typography and layout. *The Advertiser Weekly* in 1922 applauded the new appearance:

> The entire advertising is a superb example, In its beauty, its interest, its meticulous attention to detail, of the art of advertising fine products to people of cultured taste.

For much of its advertising, through to the mid-1930s, Heal's had as its advertising agency the London Press Exchange (LPE), in St. Martin's Lane; an agency perhaps better known for its work with cars and cigarettes than products where aesthetics were of prime importance,

An exhibition poster designed for Shoolbred by Paul E. Derrick advertising agency, 1928.

although it is said that Ambrose had a penchant for the former. It is possible that is how Ernest Biggs came to the firm's attention and was used for some of its posters, for he was working at LPE in the early 1920s and was later to become the agency's Art Director.

As Ambrose had advanced Heal's advertising in the early decades of the century so Anthony was to modernise it from the mid-thirties; out went Ambrose's border and bedstead and in came state of the art graphics; out went LPE and in came Pritchard, Wood & Partners. The significance of this lay not with Fleetwood Pritchard himself, but with the fact that he was the furniture entrepreneur, Jack Pritchard's brother. Jack had founded Isokon in 1929, which was to design some of the most progressive housing and furniture in the pre-war years. The Isokon reclining chair, by Marcel Breuer, was to become an epitome of modernism, sold at Heal's in its own version.

And this agency would also influence Heal's publicity through John Gloag, one of its directors, a frustrated architect who at one time had been the technical editor of the *Cabinet Maker* and was a prolific commentator on all aspects of design, a campaigner for modernism. It was Gloag who suggested the idea of getting seven 'architects' to design furniture for a Heal's exhibition, which caused some stir in the press; and it was he who was to write the foreword to the firm's commemorative booklet on the centenary of Ambrose's birth.

After the war Heal's appears to have turned to a much smaller and newer agency, Vernon Stratton, but by then its own advertising department under John Eaton (who had been at Heal's since the 1930s)

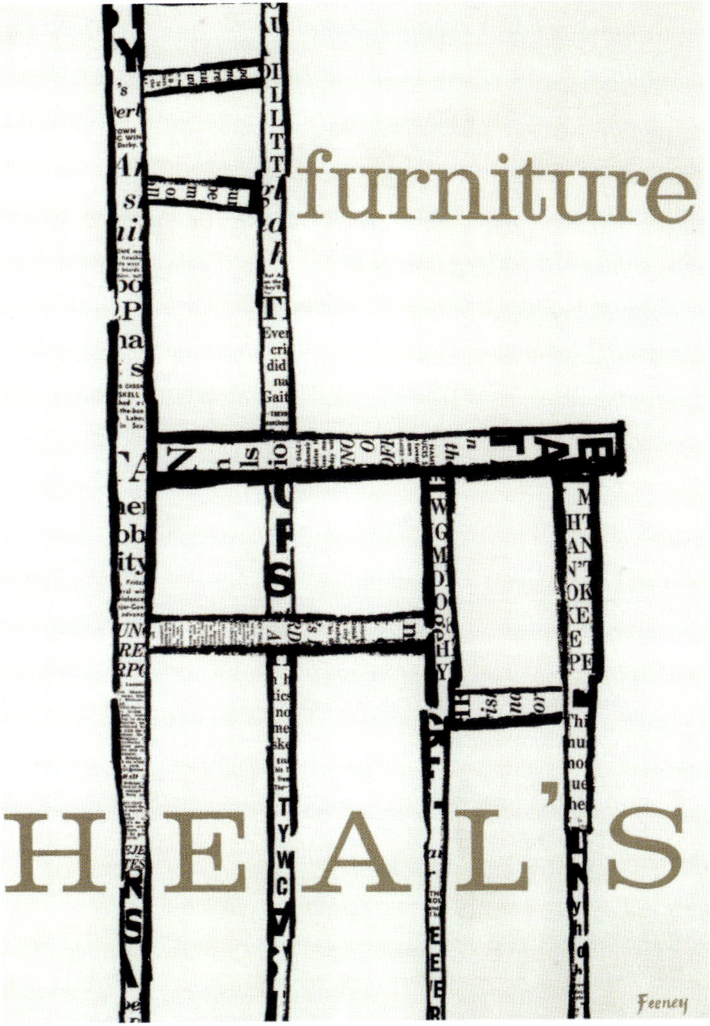

Left and above: Furniture poster designed in-house by Feeney; the same poster featured in the background of a press advert by Pritchard Wood & Partners, 1962.

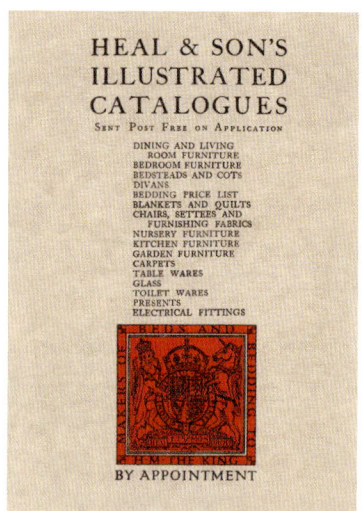

Publication listing Heal's sectional catalogues available free to customers on request, 1934.

had grown to some twenty people so possibly was carrying out a good deal of its advertising itself. Later agencies used included Roger Hughes, Gordon Proctor and the London Advertising Partnership, the last part of the biggest advertising group in Europe.

If Heal's had been an early player when it came to press advertising it was also a pioneer when it came to showing off its wares with catalogues, issuing its first in 1853. Catalogues were a means of communicating with those who, for one reason or another, could not visit the shop, as exemplified by an 1869 catalogue 'Bedsteads, Bedding and Bedroom furniture for India, China and the Colonies'. Catalogues also provided information on all the merchandise available of which only a fraction could actually be on show at any one time in the shop.

Initially Heal's catalogues were merely price lists, but over time illustrations and photos were added and copy provided, sometimes by well-known personalities who were prepared to hype the Heal's brand, as Joseph Thorp, wheeler-dealer of the printing world, Greeson White, the first editor of The Studio, and Sir Thomas Weaver and Noel Carrington, both major commentators on design. Oliver Heal quotes the Builder's Journal's comments on the catalogue in which Ambrose's furniture first appeared in 1898:

> It is rare indeed that we receive a trade catalogue which is so pleasant to handle, to look upon, to read…

Right: Prudence Maufe's elaborate 'Princess and the Pea' stand for Heal & Son, installed at the Ideal Home Exhibition of 1931.

The Heal's message of the value of good design would invariably infuse its catalogues as in a 1934 one 'Reasonable Furniture':

> In choosing the word 'reasonable' as a title we have in mind something more than the mere colloquial use of the word by which it is made synonymous with 'cheap'.

Producing catalogues was an expensive business, some London stores' catalogues running to hundreds of pages – Drages furniture store some three hundred. Eventually Heal's decided that as many recipients might only be interested in one or two categories of merchandise it would be

1937 poster publicising an exhibition at Heal's that presented replicas of what was shown at the Paris Exhibition.

more economic to produce separate smaller catalogues as for 'dining and living room furniture', 'nursery furniture' and so on.

Another publicity activity for Heal's was showing at exhibitions, and this it did from the Great Exhibition of 1851 onwards. Ambrose exhibited his designs at the Paris Exhibition of 1900, and three decades later Christopher was again showing in Paris, designing rooms in the British Pavilion for the Paris Exhibition of 1937. Heal's was the most prolific supplier of exhibits to DIA's first exhibition 'Household Things' at the Whitechapel Art Gallery in 1928 and was to be seen at most exhibitions of contemporary design in Britain in the twentieth century, including the British Art in Industry Exhibition (1935), Britain Can Make (1946) and the Festival of Britain (1951). And then there were the trade fairs as the British Industry Fairs and the Ideal Home Exhibitions. For the latter Heal's would normally have its own stand but on occasions it would also work in with other organisations as when, in 1952, it furnished the Ministry of Housing's 2 bedroom house. Heal's posters in relation to the Ideal Home Exhibition would sometimes merely be a standard poster with an added stick-on label inviting visitors to its particular stand.

Intermittently Heal's would plan to publicise itself through collaborations with other organisations, yet again hyping the events with posters. Although there are odd examples of this prior to WWII, as for the bi-centenary of Wedgwood, during the war with the British Institute of Adult Education, and immediately after the war with the new magazine *House & Garden*, most of these cooperative ventures

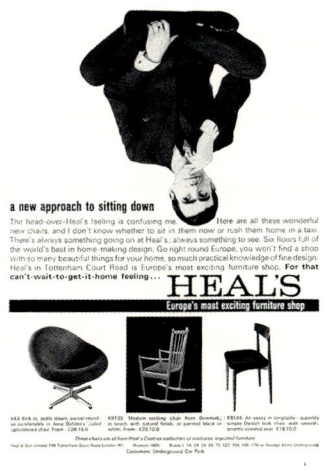

Left: Invitation to a collaborative Swedish fashion event run by Heal's and Simpson Piccadilly, undated.

Above: Advert for Heal's, from *Good Housekeeping* magazine, 1964.

 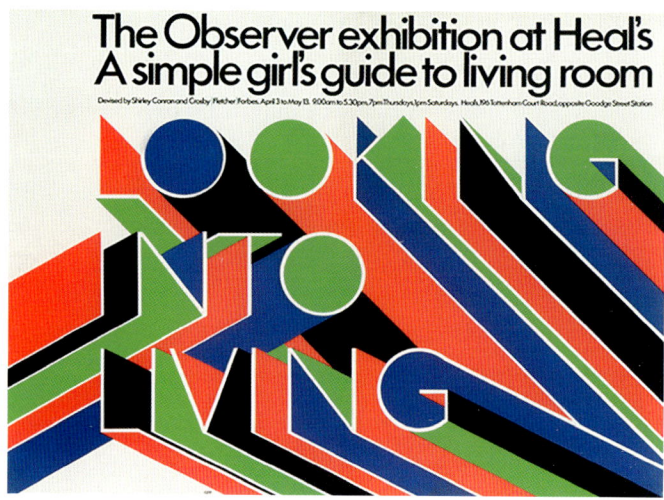

Above left: Heal's stand at the British Industries Fair 1947.

Above right: Poster designed by Alan Fletcher for an Observer exhibition at Heal's, 1967.

seem to have started from the late 60s onwards. Heal's appears to have found it profitable to feature specific manufacturers in its posters, as Meredew, Interlubke, Roset and Philips, with some smart tags as 'Heal's plugs in to Philips' and 'Roset from France, come and drink it at Heal's. And there were increased tie-ups with the press for exhibitions, as with the *Daily Mail* and the *Observer*. Other examples were with the *News Chronicle* for 'Your Elizabethan Home' on the Queen's coronation, with the *Sunday Times* for 'Gardens are for living in', and with the *Ideal Home* magazine which brought in students from Hornsey College of Art, for an exhibition 'Young Designs from Young Designers' – probably at a time when the shop was trying to shift its focus to a younger generation. A further less obviously advantageous example was a collaboration with Simpsons of Piccadilly for a Swedish week.

Right: Press advertisement from 1968 highlighting the company's policy to stock the best designs first.

Heal's advertising could generally be described as 'measured', not only because of the size of its allotted budget, but by the firm's aversion to excess. Not for Heal's the stunts of Gordon Selfridge or the swagger of Blundell Maple; at the most a featured room in *House & Garden*, a well-designed stand at a fair – and posters on the underground.

# Heal's Artists and their Posters

The artists producing posters at Heal's came from a variety of sources, some already making a name for themselves, some relatively unknown and remaining so. Ambrose, himself, had close ties with the art world – he was a regular visitor to art exhibitions (from the most traditional to the most avant garde); he owned a flat in Fitzroy Street and was familiar with some of the area's artist inhabitants, it being the territorial ground of Walter Sickert and his followers; and he had connections with the Slade School of Fine Art where both his second wife, Edith, and his cousin, Cecil Brewer, had studied. Additionally, his membership of the DIA and his relationship with Frank Pick and other of its members would have considerably extended his artistic network.

Many of the artists commissioned for posters provided only the odd one as our research has found, as F.C. Herrick with his 'Beauty in Utility' of 1927, publicising glass and pottery, possibly chosen because of the acclaim for his lion logo for the British Empire Exhibition of 1924–5; and, into the 1930s, F.H.K. Henrion for 'Sculpture in the Home', when he had only just settled in London from working with

Opposite page: Heal's catalogue artwork designed by Edward McKnight Kauffer, undated.

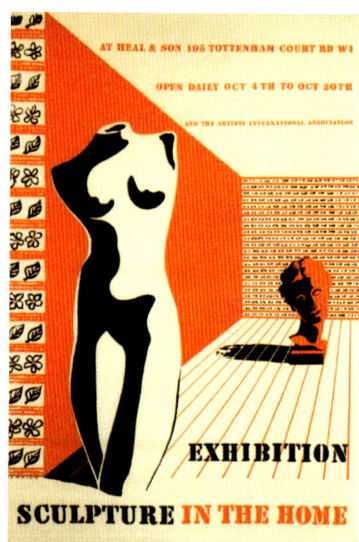

Heal's poster designed by F.H.K. Henrion for 'Sculpture in the Home' exhibition, 1945.

Paul Colin, a major French poster artist of the time. Other artists were used a number of times, such as Robert Percy Gossop, Ernest Biggs, and Ann Fisher in the 1920s, Marguerite Doring and Norman Weaver in the 1930s, and Pamela Wrightson and Charles Feeney in the 1950s and 60s.

Posters for early exhibitions in the Mansard Gallery, when it was being rented out to art groups, were inevitably made by members of the group showing – Bernard Adeney, who was President of the London Group from 1921–3 and Fred Potter its Vice-President from 1925–35. It was when these art groups showed that names of such now renowned artists as Paul Nash and Edward McKnight Kauffer became associated with, and gave kudos to, Heal's.

Some of Heal's poster artists came to them via agencies as Percy Gossop, who ran an artists' agency in Henrietta Street, and Ernest Biggs at LPE. But largely Heal's seems to have drawn from its own employees for its poster designing, as when using Rhoda Dawson, who had studied under Sickert and worked at Heal's until about 1930. Another such was Norman Weaver, who worked for the company for some five years in the 1930s, initially in its cabinet making department before his skills as a calligrapher were discovered and harnessed. And into the 1950s lettering was still seen to be key to Heal's posters with the appointment of Pamela Wrightson. Wrightson, who had been interested in calligraphy from an early age and had attended classes in it at Hampstead Garden Suburb Institute, worked for the shop for nearly twenty years, from 1947 to 1966, initially carrying out all the

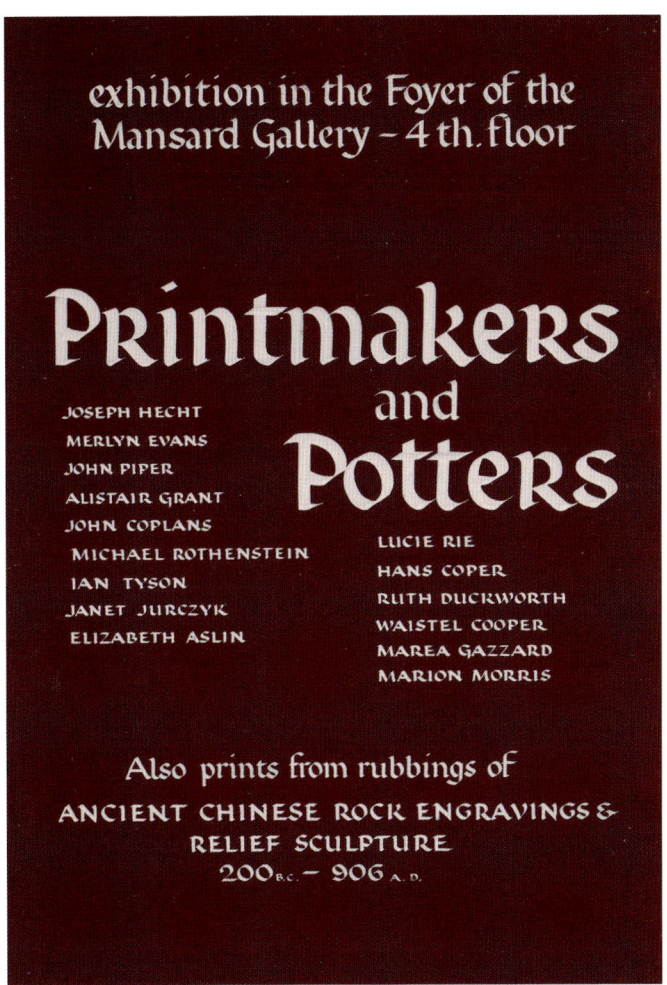

Pamela Wrightson poster demonstrating her calligraphic style.

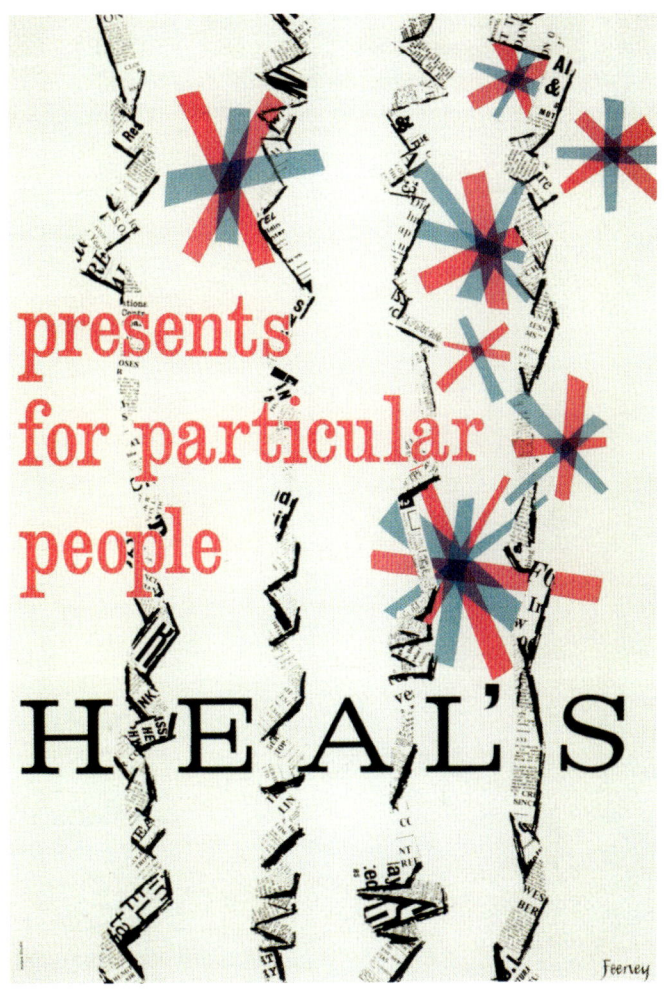

'Presents for particular people' poster by in-house designer Feeney.

lettering work herself, but eventually being allocated assistants, such was the demand for her speciality. Some posters were made up entirely with her lettering, often for hanging within the shop, whilst for others she worked with the image designer. Pamela Wrightson was not only the queen pin for Heal's lettering but became a notable figure in the Society of Scribes and Illuminators and in calligraphy internationally. Stella Cotton, who had previously worked at Heal's when she had been sent to lettering classes, reapplied when she heard that Pamela Wrightson was leaving; she continued the work of scribing and, along with David Durham, built up Heal's Graphics Department, in the late 70s to be headed up by Mike Horton.

If Wrightson ensured standards for Heal's poster lettering, the contribution of Charles Feeney to poster illustration cannot be underestimated, both for its quantity and its originality. What is so extraordinary is that he was employed as a display man, not only within the shop itself but for its stands at exhibitions at home and abroad. In 1964 a *Fourposter*, (Heal's employees' newsletter), described Feeney as looking 'exhausted but triumphant' after setting up a Heal's stand at the Frankfurt Spring Fair of that year.

Feeney had been brought up in Malta in a Service family before returning to England where he attained both a National Diploma in Design and the Associateship of the Institute of British Decorators. Before joining Heal's in 1950 he had worked in interior decorating. Feeney's out of work passion was for old clocks and watches and he probably gained favour with Prudence Maufe as in addition to his

Opposite page, top: Pamela Wrightson, Heal's calligrapher.

Opposite page, bottom: The elusive Charles Feeney, the most prolific of Heal's poster designers.

Right: This 1950s design by Feeney shows how typography became more central to poster design.

Far right: Another Feeney poster design demonstrating his versatility.

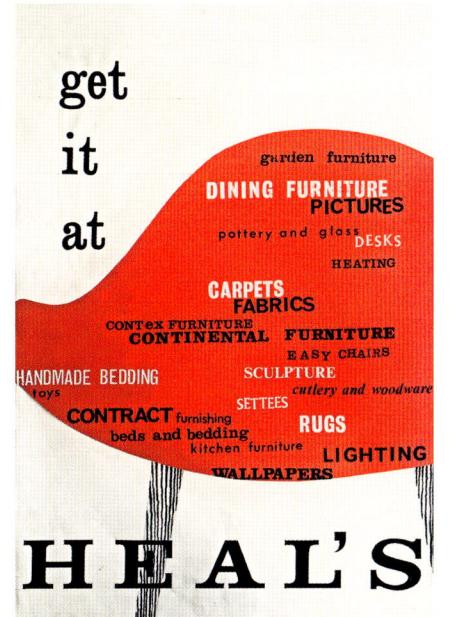

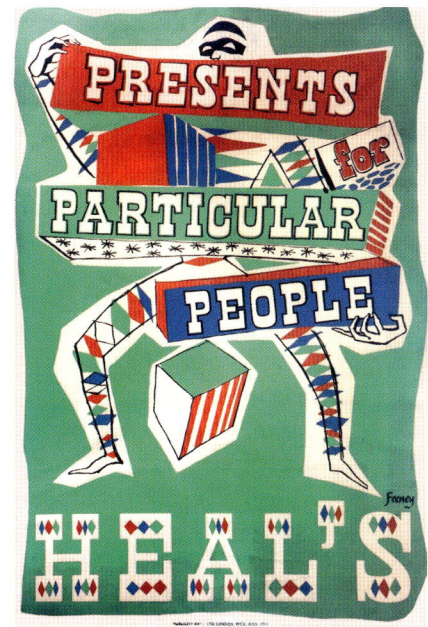

own collecting he searched for antique buckles for her collection. In spite of this historical slant to his enthusiasms Feeeney was to produce posters of the minute – colourful, light-hearted, contemporary. In all he provided more than thirty of Heal's posters, staying with the firm for the rest of his career until he retired to Spain.

Not surprisingly, when it came to design Heal's posters are to be distinguished by their lettering, which certainly smacks of modernism, although perhaps demurring from its more extravagant manifestations. Weaver's 'Winter comforts in the home' is spelt out entirely in lower case so favoured at the time by Herbert Bayer, the Bauhaus

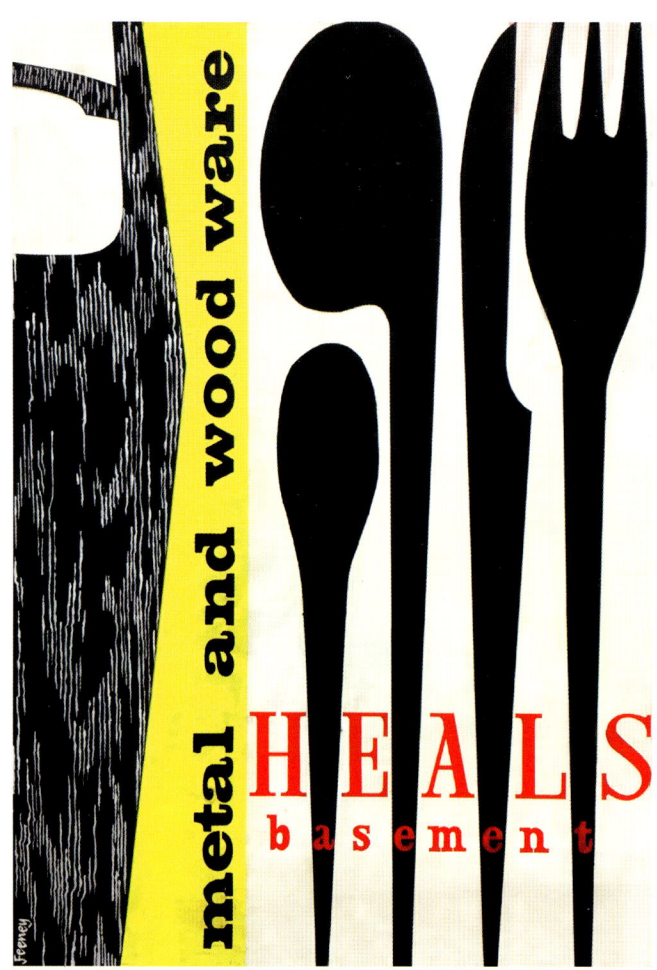

A 1959 design by Feeney for metal and wood ware, Heal's basement, reduction personified.

Poster by Norman Weaver with a first glimpse of art deco and a zebra skin rug, 1933.

Cover of a book published to mark the Weimar Bauhaus exhibition of 1923. Designed by Herbert Bayer.

typographer. But perhaps more key to Heal's posters' typographical distinction was the fact that most of its poster lettering was hand drawn; although this helped brand Heal's it inevitably led to some eccentricity. Whereas the striking red and white poster introducing Heal's 'Economy Furniture' could be said to be in contemporary sans serif type with typical pared down solid letters, no nonsense, the lettering for the poster 'Heal's for Sound Furniture' of 1927 played with in-lining , and, in others, there are squared-off apostrophes, the top of an 'A' curiously serifed, a comma added to the top of a 'g' and similar oddities. Heal's typography became even more modernistic when it became part of the design as in Weaver's 'Art in Industry' of 1935, and eventually the design itself for the posters of the 'New Design' series in the late 50s and early 60s.

From the early 1920s, when there had been a drop in sales, Heal's began to be concerned that its exceptional new brand image was actually deterring some potential customers as 'good design' became equated with 'expensive'. A notice in 1922 alerted employees to this possibility:

> …he may even be afraid to enter the attractive but supposedly expensive shop for fear he be tempted to buy what he could not afford.

The catch phrase 'Presents for Particular People', which had first appeared in Heal's advertising prior to WWI and was used

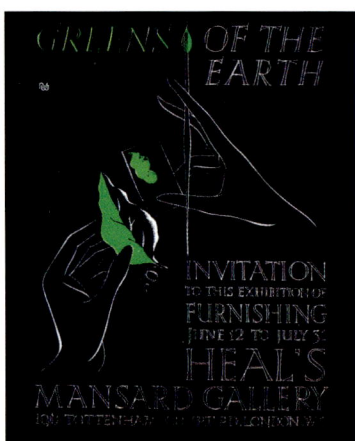

Norman Weaver's exhibition poster showing typography as part of an overall design, 1934.

intermittently through to the 1960s, further complicated the issue for although 'particular' could merely imply 'particular type of person', as bachelor or gardener, it could also be interpreted as 'special' and 'discerning' and people might not have seen themselves as sufficiently either to enter Brewer's splendid portals. This led Heal's to put out advertisements and posters reiterating that although its furniture was of the highest standards of manufacture and of the best contemporary design, it was nevertheless reasonably priced. Examples of such posters are Norman Weaver's 'Presents for pence or pounds at Heals' of 1934, and Charles Feeney's 'Furnishing to a figure' of 1953.

But generally when it came to copy for posters Heal's seems to have rarely gone in for a hard sell, for clever puns, rhymes or humour; its copy was as simple and pared down as its typography. Only into the 1980s does one find anything the slightest bit provocative or suggestive, as 'Start an Affair at Heal's'; the company was always well-mannered. With the posters appearing on the underground many of the inter-war ones had not only the address of the shop – '196 Tottenham Court Road' – but the underground station at which people should alight – 'opposite Goodge Street'. And for many of the posters 'Mansard Gallery' would be added, when people were being enticed to a special exhibition. When there were regular shows, as with 'Modern Tendencies' and 'New Designs', these words were repeated virtually as mantra. What stood out clearly, whatever the message being carried, was the word 'Heal's', usually in larger lettering, and, when it came to Feeney's later offerings, it was the only word accompanying what

Left: Another Feeney poster design taking influence from the Bauhaus design approach, 1959.

Below: The same modular design approach applied to packaging.

Exhibition poster promoting design and manufacturing, 1935.

Exhibition catalogue from 1936, design uncredited.

was being advertised, so 'Glass' and 'Heal's', or 'Upholstery' and 'Heal's'; by then was enough.

For most of the inter-war period Heal's seems to have used the old-established firm of printers, Dangerfield, which specialised in printing large coloured posters, particularly for transport operations. The name 'Dangerfield' can be seen on practically all Heal's pre-war posters. Whether the move from Dangerfield, in the 1960s, was a design or commercial decision (it had been taken over by Evershed's during the war) is not clear, but the new boy on the block was Chris Prater of Kelpra Studio. Prater and his wife, (nee Kelly, hence Kelpra), were experimental commercial silk screen printers, established in 1957. That Heal's association with the Studio was of considerably shorter duration was possibly due to Kelpra rapidly building up an international reputation as printers of 'fine' art prints, including the work of David Hockney and Bridget Riley and dropping its poster clients.

An overview suggests that Heal's posters of the 1920s slightly lacked the courage of those artists who had designed for the early exhibitions of art groups hiring the Mansard Gallery but nevertheless had begun to play around with the ratio of image to copy, in some instances breaking down the barrier between the two as in 'Heal's for Sound Furniture' and 'Heal's for Easy Chairs'; and certainly, when it came to David Preston's 'reduction', the 20s posters reduced or sometimes dispensed entirely with detail in their blocks of strong colour.

By the 1930s the posters showed altogether more freedom in design, colours even stronger, with much use of combinations of black, white and red, particularly striking in 'Contemporary Furniture, 7 Architects', 'Winter Comforts in the Home', 'Metal and Glass' and 'Heal's New Staircase', the last two particularly strong examples of poster modernism.

It was in the 1950s and 60s that light-heartedness and gaiety became more characteristic of Heal's posters, mainly with the work of Feeney. The Festival of Britain had, perhaps, started the mood – not only did furniture and furnishings become more light and bright, but there was a greater confidence in handling the relationship of image and copy; colours were less strident and were used more cleverly to direct the viewers' eye across the surface. Particularly noteworthy in this respect are the 'blues' of Feeney in 'Furnishing to a Figure' and for a poster for an exhibition of Italian furniture. 'Reduction' was still paramount, and again it is Feeney who carries the flag with his elongated cutlery in 'Metal and Wood Ware' and his triangular shaped lighting in a poster around 1959.

It was in the late 50s and early 60s that typography took over, specifically for the posters for the 'New Design' series. Just the words 'New Design' and 'Heal's' with not a glimpse of furniture, possibly showing the revitalized confidence of Heal's after the war – that would be enough to attract the design conscious.

The posters of the late 60s into the 70s and early 80s showed altogether less consistency of style as the company, possibly less sure

Right: Heal's poster to mark the Festival of Britain, uncredited, 1951.

Far right: Brian Tattersfield's poster publicising the best of French design on display at Heal's, undated.

of the commercial viability of its mission, looked here, there and everywhere for possible salvation – photography vied with graphics, strong overall design began to disintegrate, as with the over busy contents of posters for 'Buzz', and the enigmatic copy laden poster for 'Classics'. The posters seem to have become as confused as the company, with just the odd example of coherent design in the talented Brian Tattersfield's offering 'la joie en France'.

# Art Exhibition Posters

World War I found Ambrose in his striking modern building with its extensive top floor, notionally divided into a space for furniture and furnishings to be shown in arranged rooms, and another allotted for exhibitions, both seen to be possible ways of luring customers on the ground floor through the other floors of the shop; but how to make best use of the gallery?

An early exhibition in the Mansard Gallery, in 1917, actually had nothing to do directly, or even indirectly, with Heal's merchandise. Ambrose obliged his friend Frank Pick by letting him show posters that Pick had commissioned to be sent out to army billets and hospitals on the Western Front to act as 'reminders of home' for the troops. Nor did these posters actually have much to do with London Underground portraying as they did the likes of sheep on Hampstead Heath and women in the Land Army ploughing fields. It has been suggested that the show had been dreamt up by Ambrose and Pick, as a patriotic offering. The poster for the exhibition certainly demonstrated the austerity of wartime being merely in text, and entitled 'An Exhibition

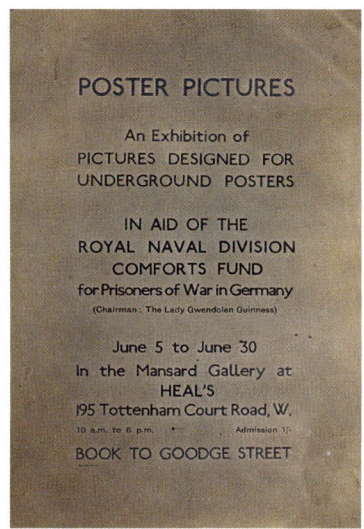

Typographic poster publicising Frank Pick's patriotic exhibition at Heal's, 'Poster Pictures', 1917.

of Pictures designed for underground posters in aid of the Royal Naval Division Comforts Fund for prisoners of war in Germany'; at the bottom 'Heal's' and 'Mansard Gallery' stood clear with the instructions to 'book to Goodge Street'; curiously the shop number is given as 195.

Ambrose went on to commission his own war-related art exhibition – 'Lithographs, efforts and ideals in the Great War', which was mounted in the Mansard Gallery in 1919. A rare reference is given to this in the Baynard Press publication *The Pleasures of Printing* telling of how Heal's invited members of the Senefelder Club (lithographers) to produce a series of symbolic pictures and that the Press's genius master lithographer, Thomas Griffits, had been of great technical help to the artists. The poster for the exhibition lists eighteen artists involved, including Edmund Dulac who illustrated 'The Freedom of Poland' and William Nicholson who proffered the pacific 'Nailing up the Door of War'. The striking image on the poster of a plane diving is in the style of Christopher Nevinson but is actually by Frank Brangwyn. *The Architectural Review*, attending the exhibition, described Heal's top floor as 'certainly the most delightful galleries in town'.

Whether the showing of art was Ambrose's primary intent or whether he fortuitously took what opportunities that arose, a precedent had been set, and for the next few years the Mansard Gallery continued to mount art exhibitions, perhaps the most notorious being that put on by the Sitwell brothers, Osbert and

Poster by Bernard Adeney for the London Group exhibition held at the Mansard Gallery, undated.

Poster by Edward McKnight Kauffer for the Group X exhibition at the Mansard Gallery, 1920.

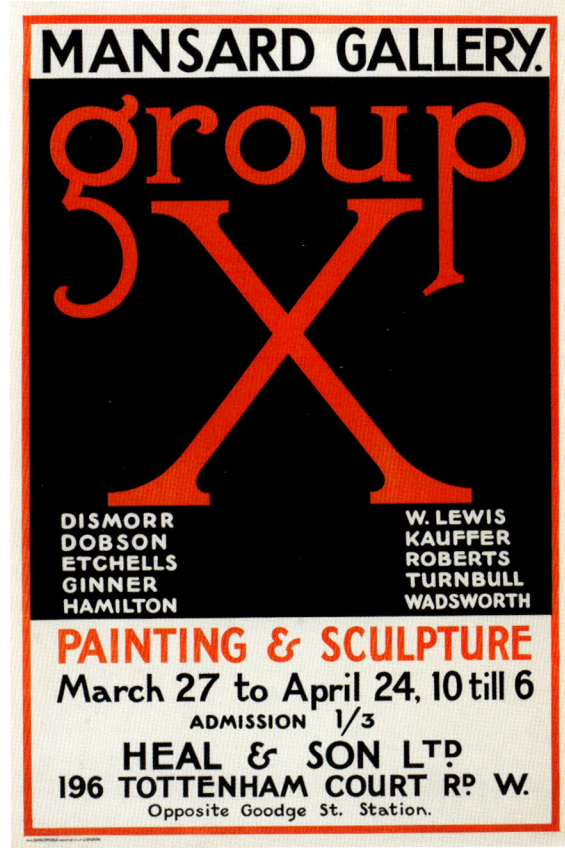

Poster for an exhibition of French Art at the Mansard Gallery, 1919.

Poster by Paul Nash for a Friday Club exhibition at the Mansard, 1921.

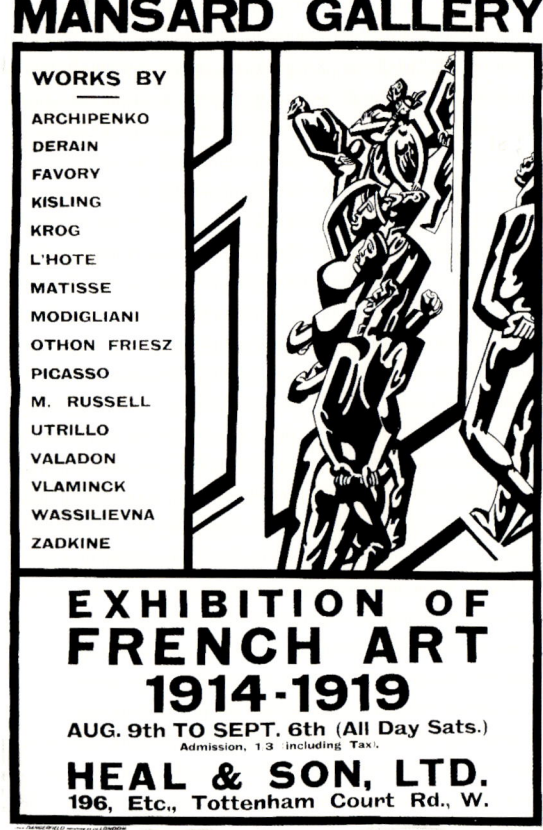

Ambrose's community of artists exhibiting works on themes of 'war' and 'peace' at the Mansard, 1918.

Sacheverell in 1919. This exhibition of French artists (and a few non-French, but working in Paris) was to link the Heal's name with the avant garde. Roger Fry had shocked Londoners with his exhibition of French painters at the Grafton Galleries in 1910, and the exhibition at Heal's was, similarly, to bring strong reactions. Sacheverell Sitwell had visited artists in Paris, including Modigliani, and along with the agent Zborowski, decided to mount a show of French artists in London and the Mansard Gallery provided just the perfect space.

In all more than 300 works by some forty artists were shown, including those of Picasso, Matisse, Leger and Soutine. The brothers, along with the great advocate of modernism, Herbert Read, attended daily, taking the entry money, selling catalogues and answering queries. James King in *The Last Moderns* has them:

> …often quieting, or trying to quiet 'protests' about the outrageous paintings and sculptures.

Whilst Mark Gertler recorded the excitement it caused with the Bloomsbury set:

> …we suddenly got a wire from Ottoline who was in London, asking us all to come up at once to go to the ballet and see a show of French pictures that were being hung at Heal's. So we rushed up.

Poster by McKnight Kauffer for London Group exhibition, 1919.

The striking poster for the Sitwell's show is by William Roberts, just emerging from his Vorticist stage. The Sitwell's were so pleased with the poster they went on to commission Roberts to illustrate some of their own publications including similar images that he produced for Edith Sitwell's magazine *Wheels*.

Of near equal notoriety were the early exhibitions of the London Group at the Mansard Gallery. Just prior to, and immediately after, WWI, London was awash with art groups, painters getting together to mount exhibitions, presenting a mixture of styles, but all in opposition to the traditional, represented for them by the Royal Academy. One group morphed into another, whilst schisms led to breakaways – such were the Allied Artists' Association, the Camden Town Group, the Fitzroy Group and the London Group. And even within the London Group there was friction between artists associated with Sickert and those around the incomer Roger Fry. Much of this warfare took place during the years the London Group exhibited at Heal's.

The London Group, formed in 1913, usually showed at the Goupil Gallery of William Merchant, and were described as including 'all sorts of modernism'. By 1916 Merchant felt uncomfortable with the Group and saw it as having pacifist elements when the war was demanding a near military like patriotism. Made homeless the Group sought shelter elsewhere which Ambrose was prepared to offer, its first showing at the Mansard Gallery taking place in 1917. The Group did not arrive quietly, cap in hand, for this exhibition included Mark

Announcement card for the 1918 exhibition of the London Group, designed by McKnight Kauffer.

Poster by Claud Lovat Fraser for an exhibition of his own work at the Mansard Gallery in 1919.

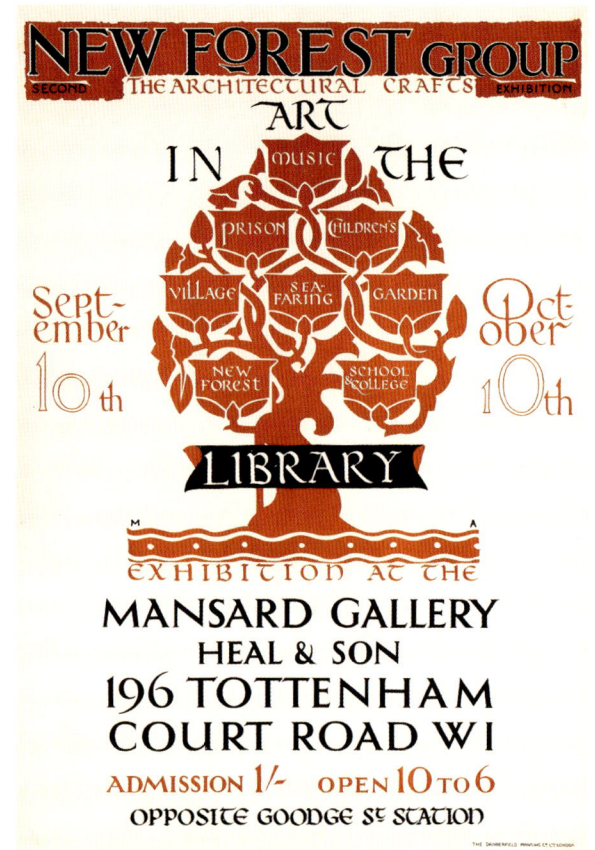

Opposite page, left: Poster by Keith Baynes for an exhibition by the London Group, 1920.

Opposite page, right: Poster by Maxwell Armfield for the second exhibition of the New Forest Group of Painters, 1924.

Gertler's 'Merry-go-Round', which attracted wide coverage in the press. Typical was the Evening News reaction to the show:

> …a shriek, a groan, a hoot, a blare, a tempest of wild rending, and most discordant noise… frightfulness in art.

The London Group held some sixteen exhibitions in the Mansard Gallery, until 1924, when it transferred to the New Burlington Galleries, where it remained for the rest of the inter-war period. With Roger Fry taking control, and the Wyndham Lewis set departing, its shows became less exciting. Ambrose's openness was such that he even gave the abrasive Lewis's short-lived Group 'X' its own showing.

Other art groups renting the Mansard Gallery in the early 1920s were the Allied Artists' Association, the New Forest Group and the Friday Club, the last started by Vanessa Bell with some of her art school friends. The Allied Artists Association, founded by Frank Rutter the critic of the *Sunday Times*, aimed to show contemporary art, including not only Lewis but Europeans, including Wassily Kandinsky.

By the late 1920s the Mansard Gallery settled down to showing mainly furniture and furnishings, but there continued to be smaller art shows in other parts of Heal's for individual artists or groups, most now long forgotten. Occasionally art would return to the Mansard as when an exhibition of the works of students from the Slade and the Royal College was mounted in 1931, including the work of the young Michael Ayrton and Rodrigo Moynihan.

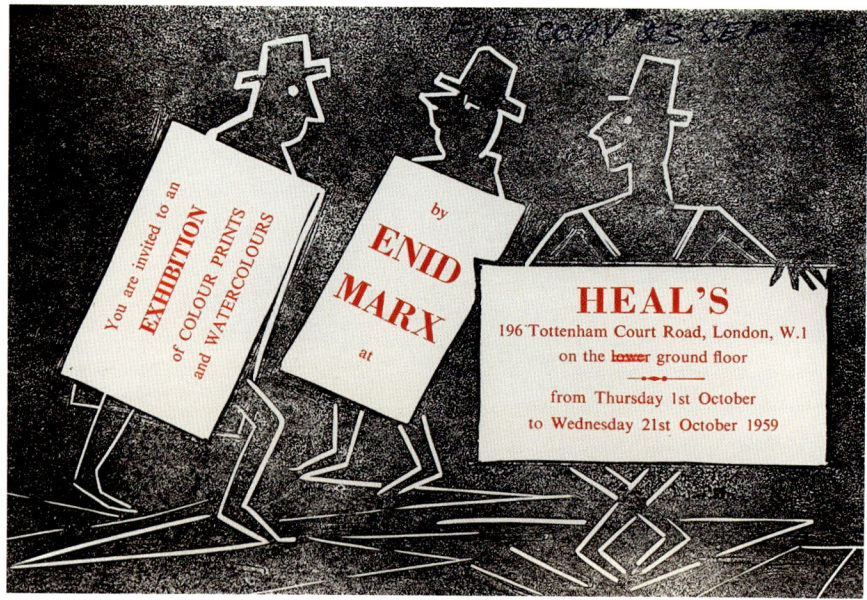

During the war the Mansard Gallery became a factory floor, while the Mansard Flat was converted into a factory canteen. But as soon as 1945 Heal's was showing an artist group's work with the radical Artists International Association's 'Sculpture in the Home'. In the post-war decades art exhibitions again were to be found on the top floor, organised by the New Art Centre of Sloane Street, showing the then contemporary generation of artists, which included Ceri Richards, Elizabeth Frink and Graham Sutherland. A curiosity in the post-war years was a 1966 exhibition of Icelandic painters (in the prescence of the Ambassador Gudmundur I. Gudmundsson), accompanied by a feast of Icelandic food and drink; and so on – Irish

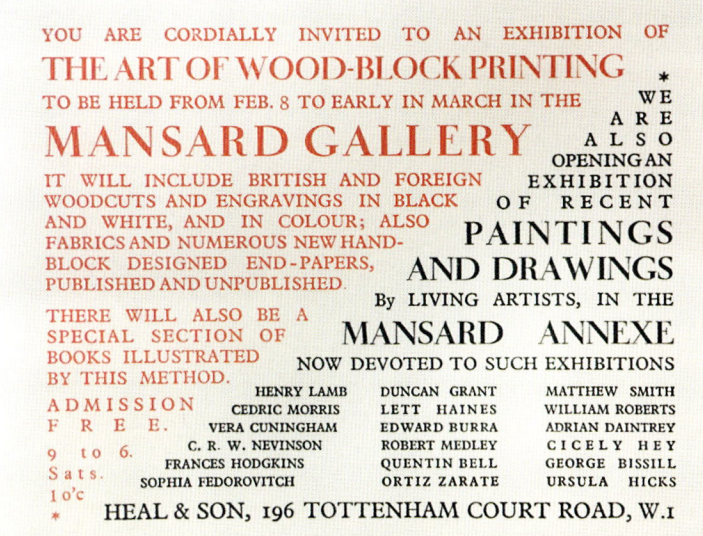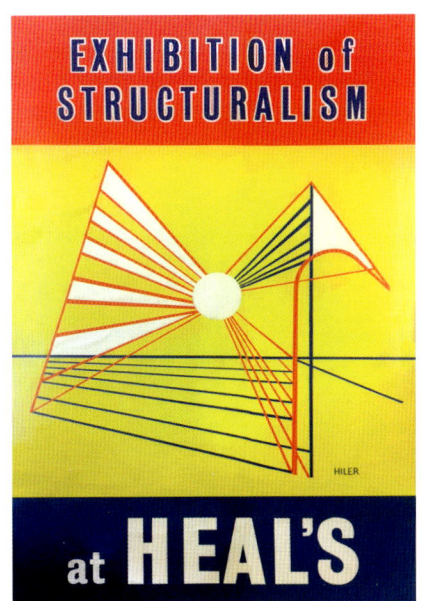

Opposite page: Invitation to an exhibition of Enid Marx prints and watercolours, 1959.

Above: Undated invite to an exhibition of wood-block printing, paintings and drawings at the Mansard Gallery.

Above right: Publicity print by Hiler for the Exhibition of Structuralism at Heal's, 1955.

food accompanying an exhibition of Irish painters etc. After the early 1930s posters for art exhibitions were rarely issued, publicity achieved largely by press advertising and invitation cards.

Although the early art exhibitions at the Mansard were not showing off Heal's merchandise, they certainly brought considerable numbers of people up to the top floor, (for some exhibitions over a thousand); and, along with their striking posters, by the likes of Paul Nash and McKnight Kauffer, marked out Heal's as a different kind of furniture shop to those around it, carrying the banner of modernism, and establishing Heal's as a company that saw art, whether painting, prints or sculpture, as essential in furnishing a home.

# Furniture Posters

Two events, in the years between the wars, were to have a major influence on furniture design – the foundation of the Bauhaus in Weimar in 1919, and the Exposition International des Arts Decoratifs et Industriels Modernes held in Paris in 1925.

Bevis Hillier mercilessly described what was emerging from the Bauhaus as 'self-righteous functionalism'; whilst Peyton Skipworth, writing from a traditionalist's point of view, was equally scathing:

> For a while the advocates of modernism, through the very clamour of their propaganda seemed to have claimed the world of art, architecture and design as their own; a New Jerusalem, a Utopia, a 'World Fit for Heroes'. At no time in the twentieth century was this self-confident, and frequently intolerant, declaration of new verities more pervasive and persuasive then during the decades that separated the two World Wars.

Although the Bauhaus only existed some fourteen years, its influence

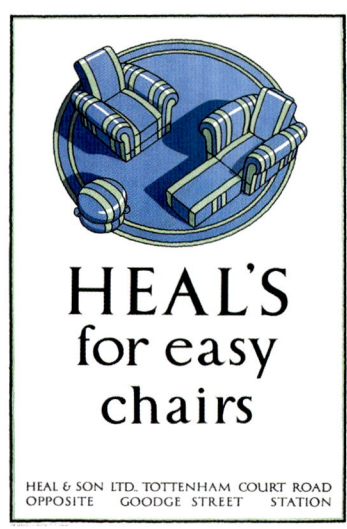

Poster by Ernst Biggs emphasising 'comfort' and featuring the Morthoe Elysian large lounge chair, c.1923.

spread across the Continent to America, aided by such emigres as Walter Gropius, Marcel Breuer, Mies van der Rohe and Laszlo Moholy-Nagy. The Bauhaus echoed William Morris in linking design to the basic needs of society and urging simplicity; and, as the D.I.A., understood the role of machinery in relation to craftsmanship and materials, in bringing good design to the populace.

The Paris exhibition brought status to the decorative arts and their designers, having on show some fifteen thousand objects for public viewing. Modernism was what it was all about, albeit the concrete, steel and glass pavilion of Le Corbusier sitting not entirely comfortably alongside the exotic expensive materials and decoration of much of what else was on display, but nevertheless sharing the general emphasis on geometric design. In hindsight, the exhibition demonstrated the schism that was to occur in 'modernism' between Corbusier's pared down functionalism and the glitzy sophistication of art deco.

Ambrose, with his roots in Arts and Crafts simplicity, and his business ethics guided by the D.I.A., steered his ship between the two. Avoiding the more radical and idiosyncratic aspects of Bauhaus design on the one hand, and the extravagant jazziness of much art deco on the other. Heal's 'Modern Tendencies' exhibitions, running from 1926 through to 1933, many of its posters designed by Marguerite Doring, indicated where his focus lay. In fact some of these posters carried a simplified image of one of Ambrose's own designs, an inlaid walnut table, which Doring placed against plain walls

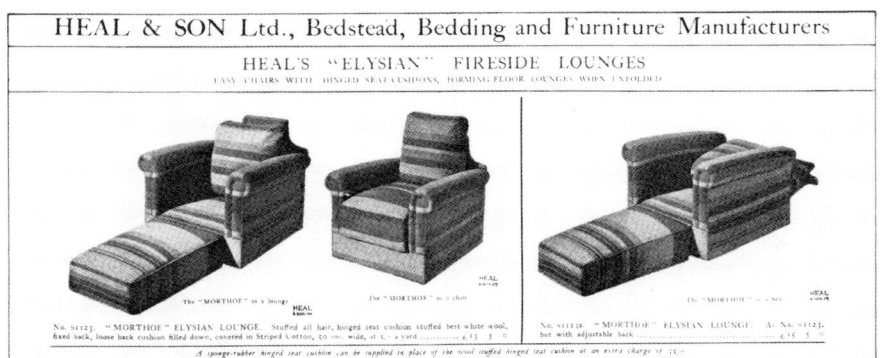

Right: Page from a Heal's catalogue showing off the 'Elysian' Fireside Lounges as featured in Ernest Biggs poster design opposite.

supporting typical early art deco lights. Deborah Cohen suggested Ambrose's dilemma in what she saw to be included in the 'Modern Tendencies' shows:

> 'Modern Tendencies' summed up the cocktail party and the aspirin, jazz and the motor car: a menacing combination of American hedonism and Teutonic conformity.

But Heal's pioneering of what most British furnishing manufacturers and retailers considered foreign and revolutionary had to be put on hold from 1929 with the Wall Street Crash and the consequent depression – critical years for Heal's survival. The company turned in every direction to find means of staying afloat – hyping its staple commodity beds and bedding and even considering redundancies. What it did do was to commission a cheaper design, Greeny's of Oxford being brought in to produce an 'economy' range. A special booklet was issued to launch this and posters were produced to give

Greiwirth poster with a standard lamp lighting up an 'easy' chair, c.1930.

R.P. Gossop poster using the 'sound furniture' tagline to boost sales, 1927.

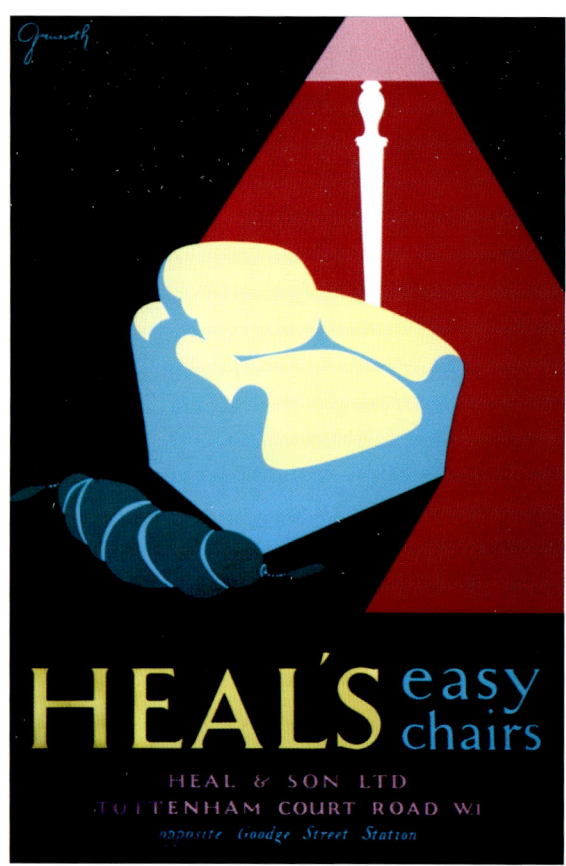

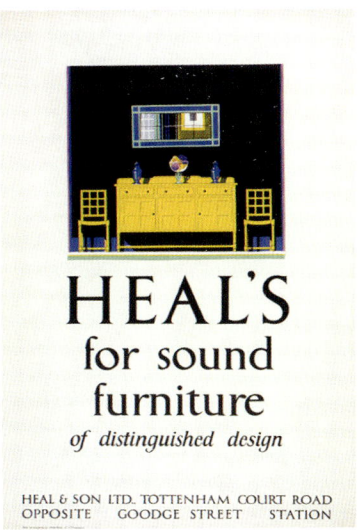

Top: Ernest Biggs poster showing off the Tilden Oak chairs under the tagline of 'sound furniture', 1925.

Above: The Tilden Oak chairs.

a suitable message. One of the most striking, entirely in typography, had the wording 'The New Type Economy Furniture' placed against a strong red patterned background. Another poster having the same focus, declared 'Economy with a Difference', suggesting that good design could still be bought, even with a tight budget.

By 1933, when a glimmer of optimism emerged, Heal's issued a booklet to 'bear witness to the new spirit that is replacing the determined gloom of 1932'. And it started issuing more positive posters with the tag 'Better Furniture for Better Times'. One designed by Arthur Greenwood, Ambrose's 'interpreter' when it came to design, showed a suite of his bedroom furniture now being manufactured back at Heal's. With the crisis abating, Heal's seems to have returned with a greater confidence to spearheading its own brand of modernism. Reflecting on what had been going on in the 1930s in British furniture design *Decorative Art* in 1940 suggested poetically:

> Fashion in furnishing bobs about like a cork on the troubled waters of the moving stream of art and architecture... tube and plywood and chrome metalwork and zebra skins and peach mirror, all cross the stage of domestic theatre, say their pieces and retire to the wings. Some come back, for others the play is ended.

Heal's poster of 1933 'Winter comforts in the Home' by Norman Weaver, certainly has the animal skin rug although the tube and the

Above: The layout of the exhibition 'Modern Tendencies' at the Mansard Gallery, 1934.

Above right: Marguerite Doring's poster for the 'Modern Tendencies' exhibition, featuring Ambrose Heal's table, 1933.

chrome are yet to make their appearance. But by 1935 Heal's was showing, at the British Art in Industry Exhibition, amongst other exhibits, a silver mirrored table, a chromium plated steel and glass table, a side table with chromium plated legs and a celluloid top, and a chromium based armchair, attributed to Ambrose – a far cry from his favoured weathered oak. In fact Heal's had held an exhibition of metal and glass furniture prior to this, in 1933, for which Norman Weaver provided the poster, one of the best, which was selected by the Arts Council and Victoria & Albert Museum for an exhibition at the Heywood Gallery in 1980 as typifying the period.

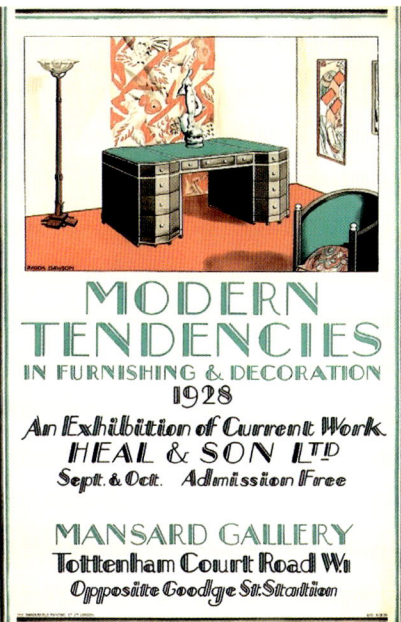 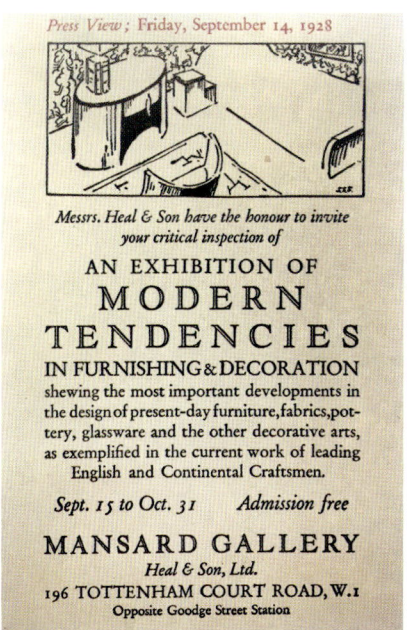

Above right: Poster design by Rhoda Dawson for the 'Modern Tendencies' exhibition, 1928.

Above far right: Invitation to the 'Modern Tendencies' exhibition, 1928.

Perhaps Heal's most courageous show of modernism was in its exhibition 'Contemporary Furniture, 7 Architects', mounted in 1936. Shoolbred and Waring & Gillow both had had modernist exhibitions before the Depression, the latter particularly memorable with its then studio director, Serge Chermayeff's luxurious furniture; but neither store seem to have had a long term commitment to such exotic ware. '7 Architects' was to have an altogether more lasting influence, for it not only included the work of some of the most exciting up-and-coming designers of the time, but had some of the earliest pieces from Christopher Heal. The store appears to have been particularly

Right: Page from a 1953 catalogue showing how two rooms can be fully furnished for two people for £395.

TWO ROOMS FOR TWO PEOPLE FOR £395

Living Room

*The idea of selling house packages of Heal's style had started in the Thirties, when Prudence Maufe organised special displays of the new economy furniture. The Furnishing to a Figure exhibition*

opportunistic in catching for the exhibition Marcel Breuer in the very short window of his stay in London before he left for America. Heal's version of Breuer's Isokon chair, was to become a classic, and his furniture continued to be sold by Heal's as, for example, when it was featured in such exhibitions as the 1939 'Furniture for small homes'. The poster for the exhibition is not attributed, but has the same all-black background to the 1933 'Heal's New Staircase' and to 'Economy with a difference' the latter designed by Dunn. By the late 1930s Heal's was not only awash with metal and chrome tubes, including the selling of Pel products, but afloat with new woods and new ways with wood, being Finmar's first customer for imported Alvar Aalto classics.

Left: 1930s poster promoting the idea that good design is not necessarily expensive, uncredited.

Below: The Heal's lounge chair featured on the 'Pence or Pounds' poster design.

Above: Invitation card for an exhibition of metal and glass furniture, 1933, uncredited.

Right: Poster by Norman Weaver for the metal & glass furniture exhibition.

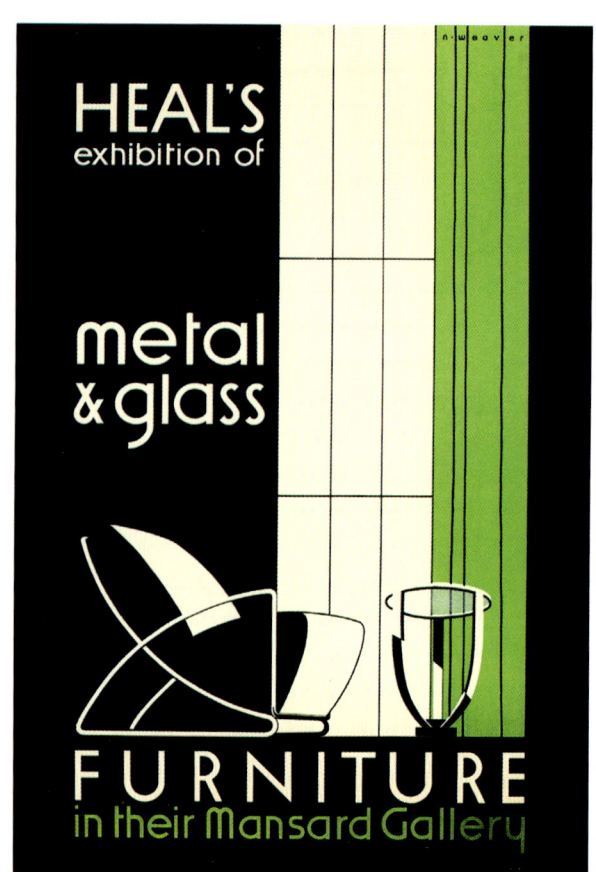

Poster for 'Contemporary Furniture by 7 Architects', exhibition at the Mansard Gallery, 1936.

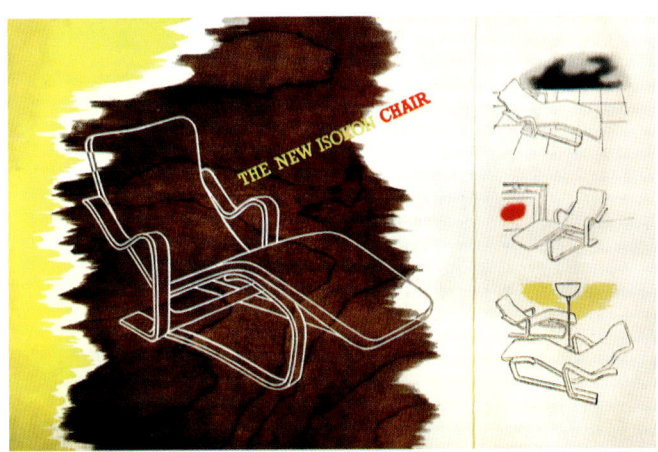

Heal's catalogue showing Marcel Breuer's 'Long Chair' for Isokon, 1935. And a photograph of Breuer's chairs in action.

Left: Poster for 'New Type' economy furniture, 1932, uncredited.

Below: Feeney poster stressing that good design need not be expensive, 1953.

Catalogue cover design with an illustration by 'dunn', 1933.

Catalogue cover design by Norman Weaver, 1934.

### SYCAMORE AND WALNUT BEDROOM

WARDROBE, C1033; on walnut base, chromium handles; shelf and rod for coathangers, 4 ft. wide; 6 ft. high .. £31 10 0
DRESSING-TABLE, C1033; adjustable mirror; 3 drawers; pink mirror-glass top; 3 ft. 6 in. wide .. 26 5 0
CHEST OF DRAWERS, C1033; 3 long and 2 short drawers; chromium plated handles, 3 ft. wide by 3 ft. high .. 22 10 0
BEDSIDE CUPBOARD, C1033; with bookspace over .. 8 17 6
BEDSTEADS, C560; fitted iron frames, 3 ft. wide .. each 14 0 0
CHAIR, C1033; stuffed seat and back, covered in woven cotton 3 3 0
DRESSING STOOL, C1033; seat covered in woven cotton .. 5 5 0
TABLE LAMP, E2683; any colour; celastoid shade complete 1 10 0
VASE, P5568; Trebarum ware; hand thrown; 10 in. high .. 12 0

Stand No. 29, Ideal Home Exhibition, 1934

### THE HIGHBROW

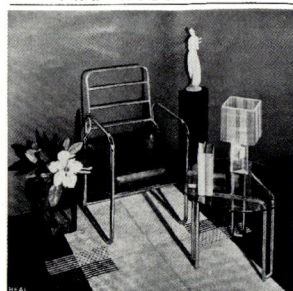

ARMCHAIR, MW2007, chromium-plated steel; hinged back; 2 cushions in red rexine (back one not shown) £9 9 0
TABLE, MW1882, chromium-plated steel; plate glass top; 1 ft. 6 in. high by 2 ft. diameter .. 4 15 0
METAL FURNITURE. Heal's have many examples of this new and interesting furniture for bedrooms, living rooms, etc.
FIGURE, P7652, 'Princess'; by Schliepstein; white porcelain; 18 in. high .. 5 17 6
LAMP, F2493, square mirror-glass base; blue & white tubular-glass shade (also in amber); 15¼ in. high .. 4 4 0
BOOKENDS, P9239, crystal glass cubes:—
2¾ in. 17/6 the pair; 3 in. 21/- the pair
FLOWER TANK, P12627, green glass; (Size. 11½×6½ 3½) 10 in. .. 15 0
RUGS*, F2272, velvet pile; modern design in black & white (not shown); 5 ft. by 3 ft. .. each 1 11 0
*Foreign Make

Opposite page, main image: Hand-drawn poster by Arthur Greenwood for his 'Better Times' furniture in sycamore and walnut, 1934.

Opposite page, top: Catalogue page showing Greenwood's furniture for 'Better Times', c.1934.

Opposite page, bottom: Catalogue page titled 'The Highbrow', with chromium-plated steel furniture.

Above right: 'Contemporary Furniture' advertisement from *Ideal Home* magazine, 1952.

But as at the Depression, Heal's had, yet again, to rein in its pioneering, with the onset of war. Christopher was away serving his country, and much of Heal's was given over to producing parachutes, protective clothing, and the like, for the war effort. In 1942 the Government introduced its Utility Furniture Scheme with its rationing and prescribed furniture designs. Although Heal's was registered to manufacture these, it was severely restricted as to what it could and could not make, and to whom it could sell. Exhibitions and posters were largely put on hold, although a couple of posters, merely typographic, tell of a Heal's collaboration with The Housing Centre, The National Council of Social Service and the British Institute of Adult Education for a show – 'Country Life & Country Needs', and another, with the Institute – 'Design for Living', both mounted towards the end of the war, looking ahead to peacetime.

'Contemporary Furniture' poster by Charles Feeney, 1948.

Feeney poster with 'New Designs' now replacing 'Contemporary', 1954.

Another 'New Designs' poster by Feeney in the same style as the previous year, 1955.

In spite of rationing and austerity continuing through to the early 1950s, the exuberant spirit afield after the war, the optimism of the nation with the new millennium promised by a reinvigorated government, and the design renaissance heralded by the Festival of Britain and the newly formed Council of Industrial Design – all were contagious. The 1950s and 60s proved heady days for Heal's. Christopher had returned from service and his, Clive Latimer's and Andrew J. Milne's designs were being manufactured – years for which Prime Minister Harold MacMillan declared we 'never had it so good'. 'Contemporary' came to replace 'modern' – and Heal's furniture posters, largely by Charles Feeney, were to be some of its best.

And it was in the late 1950s that Heal's began to import continental furniture in a big way, setting up CONTex as its agency, a move that was to prove something of a cuckoo in the nest. The word 'continental' was to be seen in the poster 'Get it at Heal's', and before the 1950s were out continental furniture began to have its own posters, some countries imports being represented separately as Scandinavia and Italy, A crescendo of publicity came at the end of the decade with Heal's declaring itself 'Europe's most exciting furniture shop'. By 1960 Heal's had become so confident in its pioneering of European merchandise that to celebrate its 150 years of existence it commissioned six countries to produce designs that were then manufactured at Heals and on sale in the shop. Heal's invited a 'group leader' for each country – an architect, furniture designer or interior decorator – to select suitable young designers, so, for instance, Professor Gio Ponti

This page and opposite page, main image: Various posters by Feeney publicising Italian (1951), Continental (1955) and Scandinavian (1957) furniture at Heal's.

Heal's poster promoting 'Europe's most exciting furniture shop', undated.

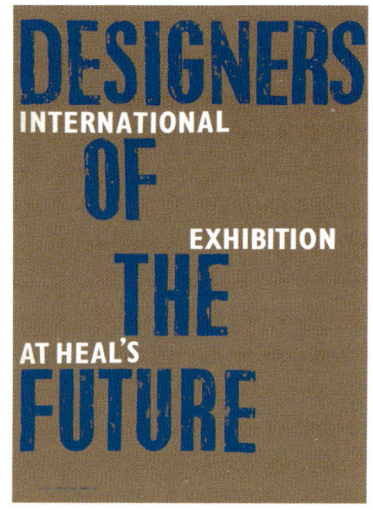

Above: Poster design by Antoni promoting the 'Heal's Have Denmark' exhibition, 1968.

Above right: 'Designers of the Future' exhibition poster, undated.

was responsible for the Italian offerings. The countries involved were Italy, Germany, Switzerland, Sweden, Norway and Finland, whilst Christopher chose the British designers. The European theme continued through the next two decades, although with less frequency, with the odd poster as 'Finland in England', 'Heal's Europe '73' and Brian Tattersfield's jolly 'La joie en France' in 1982.

Then came Buzz – Heal's last ditch attempt to catch up with what was going on in Carnaby Street – the youth market, already successfully magnetised by Habitat. Susanna Gooden quotes Oliver,

Above: Poster for Heal's exhibition with *Ideal Home* magazine and Hornsey College of Art, c.1960s.

Above right: Poster for 'Buzz at Heal's', undated and uncredited.

Anthony's son, who had become Managing Director in 1980, admitting that Heal's had lost the fight, as it had sacrificed its clear missionary image to aim for short term volume sales through 'street' popularity. One of the few Buzz posters says it all – crowded with everything the shop could think of from its merchandise that might appeal to the young, merely stolidly laid out in rows, without energy or fun, no real sincerity of purpose and certainly no Buzz.

# Etcetera

Although Heal's was founded as a maker of bedding and bedsteads, by the end of the nineteenth century not only had it extended its range of merchandise to furniture for most of the rooms of a house, it had added 'furnishings'. Carpets were early additions, and by the start of WWI, 'chintzes and printed linens' were on sale and a pottery and glass department had been installed. Gossop's poster of 1928 showed that by then Heal's was offering furniture and furnishings for the whole house.

### China and glass

Not all the 'etceteras', the additions to furniture and bedding, seem to have warranted posters, presumably a matter of how key a product's contribution might be to Heal's income. The group most frequently seen on posters was 'pottery and glass', invariably paired together. Heal's china and glass department was officially opened in 1910 and merited its own posters from time to time through the 1920s and 30s,

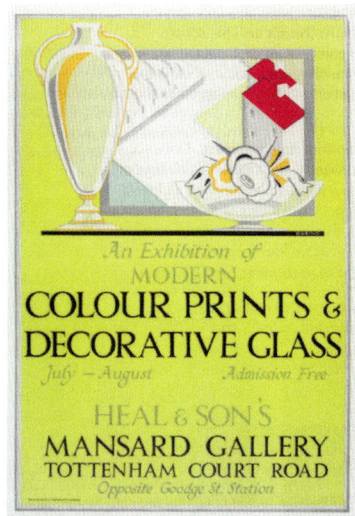

Poster by Marguerite Doring for a special exhibition at the Mansard Gallery, 1926.

and then, after a lapse during the war and the years immediately after, it again featured in posters of the 1950s and 60s. A Mass Observation Survey commissioned for Heal's by Pritchard, Wood & Partners in 1959 found 'pottery and glass seem to be outstandingly thought of as a Heal's speciality'.

Ambrose is said to have had an early influence on purchases as when, after seeing an early Wedgwood pattern, he commissioned its reproduction for the shop; and again, having been impressed by a display of glass at the 1923 Goteborg Exhibition, he made Heal's a pioneer in importing Swedish glass to Britain. By 1925 Heal's felt able to claim in a catalogue:

> Heal's China Department contains a choice of the best that is being done in modern pottery and glass. In addition to articles for use, both for the table and for the toilet, there is a permanent exhibition (of which pieces are continually changing) comprising vases, bowls and other decorative pieces and likewise notable pottery figures by British and Continental artists.

By the mid-1930s Heal's was selling glass not only from Sweden and from such English manufacturers as Pilkington, Whitefriars and Pyrex, but from Czechoslovakia, Holland and France as well.

The man who was to build up the reputation of the department was Harry Trethowan, described by some as genial and sociable, by

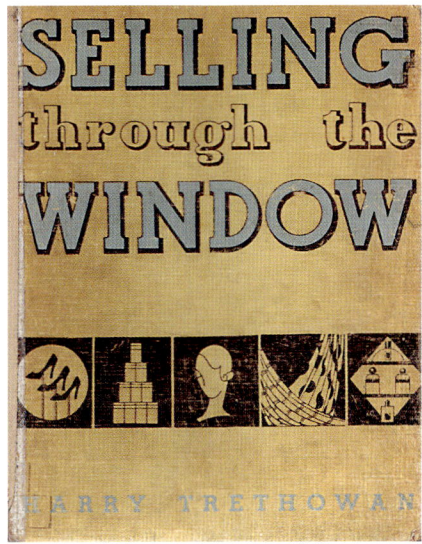

Above: Heal's China and Glass Department, 1935.

Above right: Harry Trethowan's book on store display, 1935.

others as pompous. Trethowan was actually responsible not only for his department but for display throughout the building, although perhaps feeling a partiality for pottery and glass in that he, himself, had been something of a potter at one time (having one of his pots manufactured by what was to become Poole Potteries).

Trethowan, Cornish born, had been apprenticed to Criddle & Smith, the 'Complete Home Furnishers' of Truro. He joined Heals' in 1913 and remained there until his retirement in 1953, in charge of display and buying. Trethowan was a modernist. Pronouncing at a DIA meeting 'prestige means selling for tomorrow and next year, not merely for to-day'. In an article entitled 'Modern British Pottery Design' he wrote of the potter:

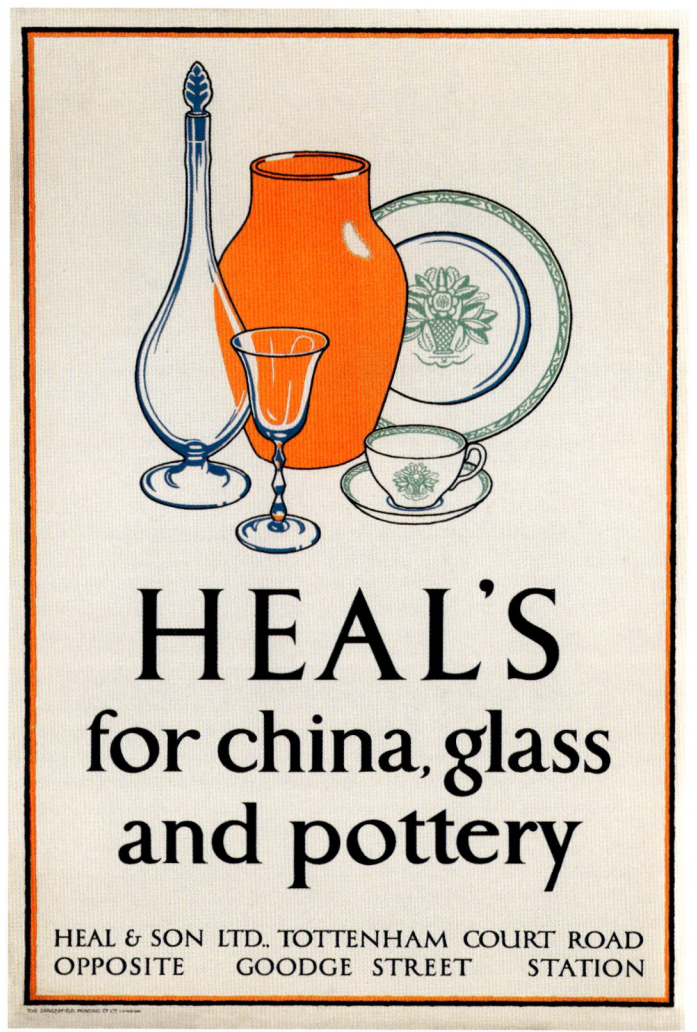

Above: Poster by Feeney promoting glassware at Heal's, 1960s.

Right: General poster for china, glass and pottery department, 1920s.

Above: A selection of ornamental vases designed by Keith Murray.

Right: Poster for Pots & Weaves exhibition featuring one of Murray's vases, 1937.

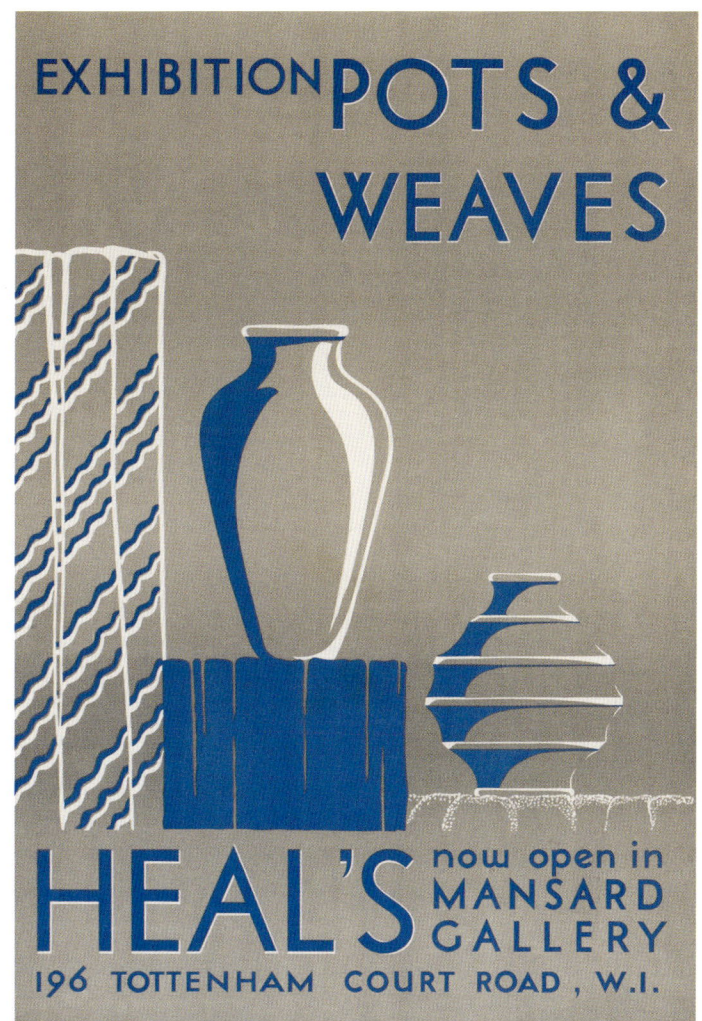

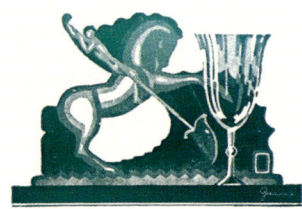

Invitation card for 'Modern Ceramics & Colour Prints' exhibition at the Mansard Gallery, 1930s.

One who eventually becomes steeped in the process of manufacture and is then capable of expressing himself in clay that in form and fashion shall be characteristic of the twentieth century.

He could well have had in mind Keith Murray, who designed for Wedgwood and whose pottery appears in a poster for an exhibition of Pots and Weaves in 1929. And from an invitation card for 'Crockery, its place in the home and its problems in the shop', it would seem that Trethowan occasionally took on Heal's educational role by giving lectures on his merchandise (illustrated by lantern slide). It was he who was to champion, from the 1920s, contemporary glass from France and Italy as well as from Sweden's Kosta and Orrefors. Trethowan was here there and everywhere, ensuring the name Heal's was ever in the public eye, with his involvement with DIA, being Vice-President of the China & Glass Retailers Association in 1927, and the President of the National Display Association in 1938. He was also on a number of exhibition committees and was a member of the Government's Gorrell Commission on Art and Industry in 1934. In 1935 he collected together his thoughts on display work in a book *Selling through the Window*, modestly only including one example from his own department in Heal's.

Post-war posters for Heal's pottery and glass show it to be drawing its products from across Europe and it was also selling

Right: Poster for inter-war exhibition at the South Mansard gallery focused on 'Danish Table Settings', 1939.

Far right: Poster showing pâte blanche pottery, popular at the time, 1926.

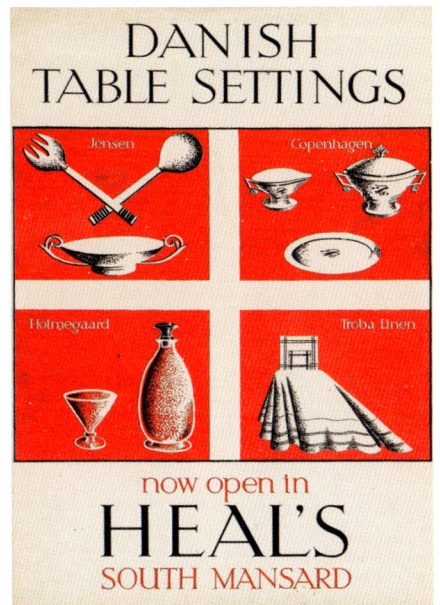
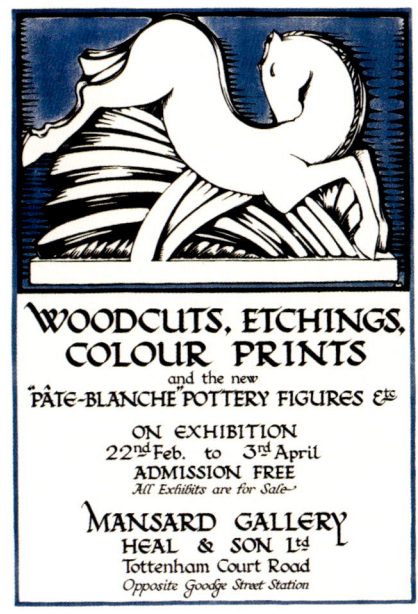

pottery from European immigrants as Lucie Rie and Hans Coper. Perhaps as a tribute to Trethowan there was a Cornish pottery exhibition of Troika pottery, which had a flash of popularity in the 1960s; Trethowan had died in 1960.

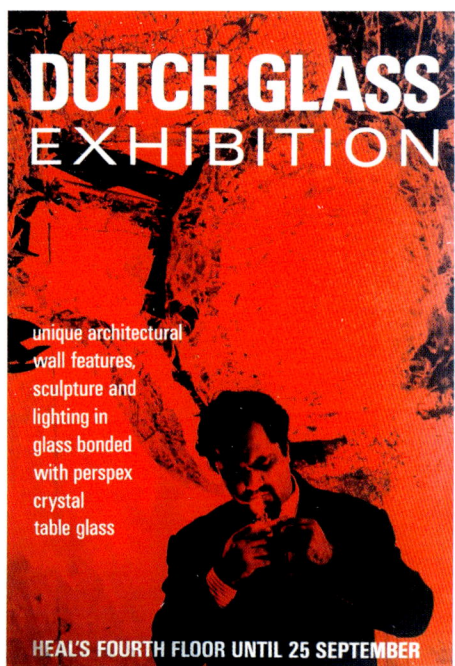

Above: Feeney poster for pottery, glass and cutlery, 1958.

Right: Poster and catalogue marking a Dutch Glass exhibition at Heal's, undated.

### Children's furniture and toys

Merchandise for children was available from Heal's from the mid-nineteenth century when its bedstead range included cribs and cots and bassinets. By the turn of the century a full range of nursery furniture was on sale; and into the 1930s there were fully furnished day and night nurseries along with suitable pictures for the nursery walls. It is not clear when the selling of toys was taken seriously but the 1919 exhibition of 'New toys for sale' could well have been a kick start.

Ambrose had visited Claud Lovat Fraser and noticed his and his wife, Grace's collection of old toys. Not only did this result in a selling exhibition of toys in the Mansard Gallery with a display of some of the Lovat Fraser collection, organised by Grace with her husband providing the poster, but Lovat Fraser was commissioned to design toys for the shop. Skipworth & Webb in their tribute to Lovat Fraser described these as 'witty, simple and colourful'.

In 1924 the Little Gallery was set up on the second floor to sell children's furniture, toys and pictures, managed in the 1920s by Dodie Smith, later to become well-known for her writing of *One Hundred & One Dalmatians*. This also sold pictures and other decorative items. Heal's described the pictures offered to 'a discerning public', as 'relatively unpretentious' prints and woodcuts… 'by artists of repute'.

Toys were to have a renaissance at Heal's in the 1960s when Kristin Baybars worked in the department. She became a maker of toys, including Humpty Dumpty for television's Play School, Heal's

Inter-war poster for opening of new department, c.1924.

Above right: Example of Heal's children's toys from their catalogue.

sold her toys along with those of other young toy designers making their names, such as John Gould (who later taught toy and furniture design at the London College of Furniture).

Corin Hughes-Stanton writing in *Design* in 1965 applauded Heal's ventures:

> Until a few years ago there were virtually two kinds of toy – bad toys and seriously educational toys… a change practically solely due to Heal's.

 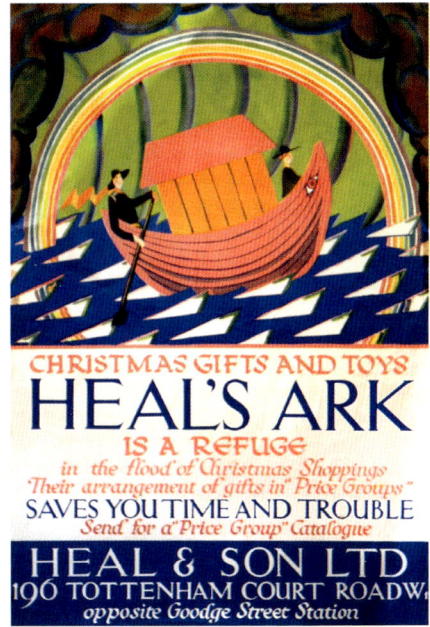 

Above: Poster for a nursery exhibition designed by S.A. Watkins, 1938.

Above centre: Christmas poster for the toy and gift department, c.1930s.

Above right: Poster by Claud Lovat Fraser for an exhibition of toys arranged by Lovat Fraser himself.

Presumably toys were a sufficient bait for customers for Heal's to put on several special exhibitions, each with their own poster, as in 1938, with a poster by S.A. Watkins, and in the 1960s 'Living with Children', at one time providing a Saturday Playgroup possibly to attract parents beyond the Little Gallery.

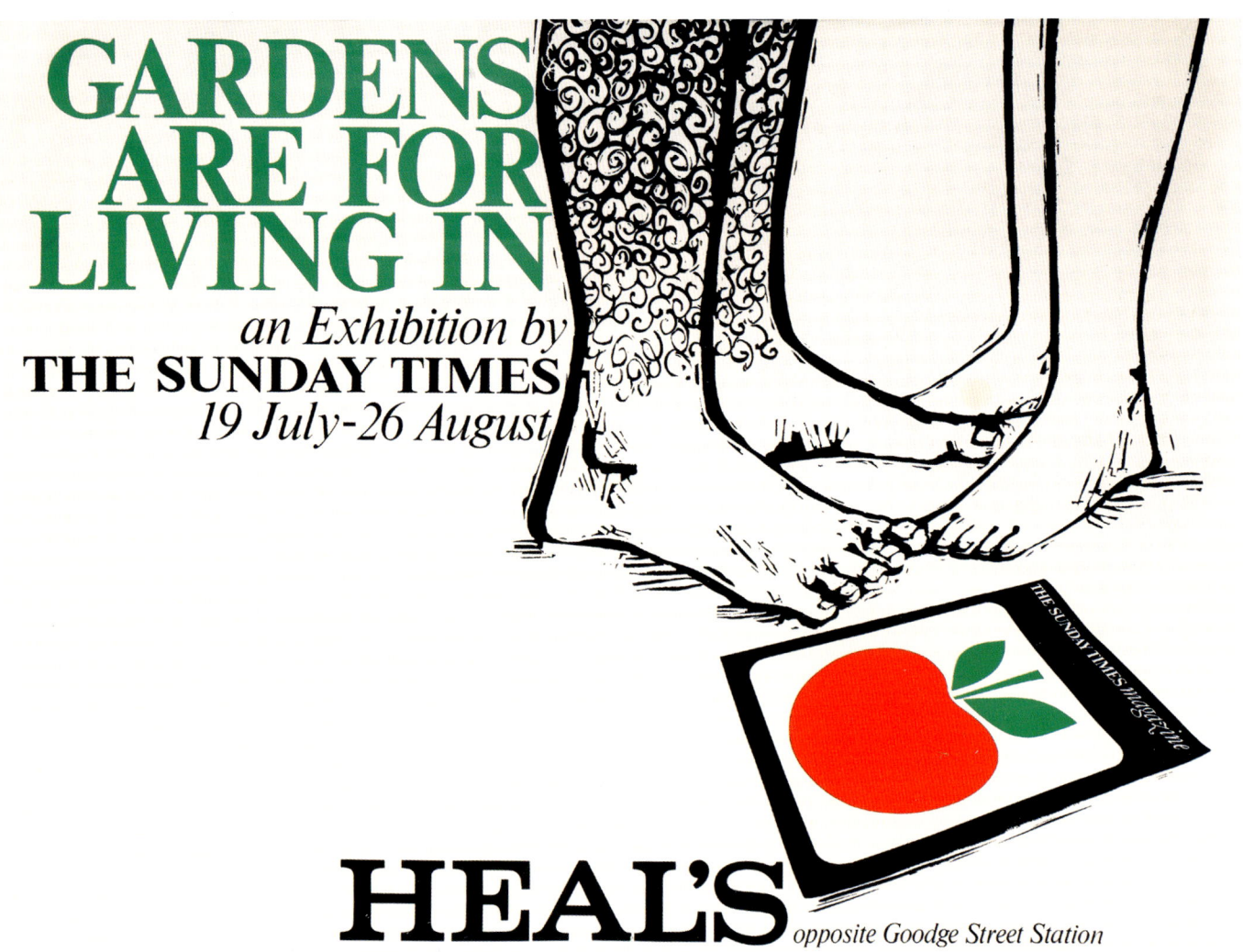

Opposite page: Poster for joint garden exhibition with *The Sunday Times*, 1960s.

Above: A selection of Heal's furniture for the garden, including a Lutyens style bench.

Above right: Poster for early garden furniture exhibition, designed by Ann Fisher, 1921.

### Garden furnishings

From as early as 1921, Heal's was making a special feature of its garden furniture, which was on show in the basement. In the early years of the twentieth century, with the extension of the Metropolitan Line, Metroland emerged – London spread itself into Buckinghamshire, Hertfordshire and Middlesex. And it was in the first decades of the twentieth century that Raymond Unwin's Hampstead Garden Suburb and the Garden Cities movement developed. Heal's had furnished the Letchworth Cheap Cottage Exhibition in 1905. All of this meant low density housing, either detached or semi-detached, each dwelling having its own plot of land.

Heal's appears to have fairly quickly appreciated these developments as seams to be mined, issuing special catalogues as 'Presents for Particular People – The Helpful Gardener'; and mounting

Above right: Two garden posters for Heal's designed by Betty Cooke, 1938 and 1939 respectively.

targeted exhibitions as its 'Garden furniture & decorations' in 1921, and again in 1938, with a charming poster by Betty Cooke of intertwined reclining garden chairs. It was Heal's who supplied a garden and a terrace chair to the Homes and Gardens section of the Festival of Britain. Even into the 80s Heal's was featuring garden furniture in posters, possibly unconsciously revealing who Heal's really considered its main customers, with the likes of croquet sets and picnic baskets.

Left: Charles Feeney poster design for Heal's garden furniture, 1966.

Above: An early Heal's poster promoting garden furniture, printed by Dangerfield, undated.

Poster for Serbian rug exhibition at Heal's Gallery, 1920.

### Textiles

Textiles were another 'etcetera' for Heal's, although bolsters, pillows, mattresses and carpets were being sold as accessories to bedsteads from its early days. It mounted a number of exhibitions in the 1920s showing folk textiles – Serbian rugs, or, vaguely, 'Woven fabrics', along with its own curtaining, each show having its own poster. In the 1935 British Art & Industry Exhibition Heal's contributed both carpets and rugs, one by Lady Heal herself! In 1939 Heal's was circulating some three hundred firms offering them fabrics suitable for window blackouts (compulsory during the war). Yet there are no posters for the fabrics that were going to earn Heal's its reputation as influencing public taste with avant garde designs – in the 1920s and 30s designed by the likes of Marion Dorn, Marian Pepler and Marianne Straub; and in the 1950s and 60s by Lucienne Day.

In 1941 it had set up a subsidiary – Heal's Wholesale & Export Ltd. to sell its surplus wartime material. This was renamed Heal's Fabrics, and was headed up very successfully by Tom Worthington. It was he who was to commission Lucienne Day, although being quite skeptical at first about whether her spikey offerings were saleable. She was to produce four to six designs annually for Heal's, through to the 1970s, her early 'Calyx' for the Festival of Britain becoming a best seller.

It remains something of a mystery as to why these post-war avant garde designs neither merited special exhibitions nor posters.

Poster by Marguerite Doring promoting 'fadeless' curtains, c.1923.

'Needle Shuttle and Maul' poster by Pamela Wrightson, 1950s.

Feeney at his most 'reduced', c.1959.

## Lighting

Lighting was one of the more minor etceteras, rarely featuring even as an accessory in catalogues or advertisements let alone posters until the early 1930s. An electrical department was set up in 1931, initially managed by Anthony. The first special catalogue on lighting was issued in 1933. 30s lighting at Heal's, whether for ceiling, table, walls or floor, was characterized by a near total lack of ornamentation, but a good deal of silver, either in chrome or silvered metal. Globes were the fashion, either plain or simply fluted.

Posters for lighting do not appear to have been produced until the 1950s, when Feeney designed two, one in 1953 for a Mazda exhibition, and one in 1959/60, perhaps the most pared down of all Heal's posters. Paul Reilly, then Head of the Council of Industrial Design, wrote somewhat scathingly of the modernism of the lighting in Heal's 1961 'New Design' exhibition:

> Internationalism. I am the first to welcome the import of good foreign ideas… but the balance has been lost; there were too many German light fittings for my taste and several of them were too strident and obtrusive for comfortable viewing.

Yet again Heal's was ahead of the flock!

A modernist poster for an exhibition of 'Light & Glass' at Heal's Mansard Gallery, 1934.

'Lighting to Measure', Feeney poster for a joint exhibition with Mazda, 1953.

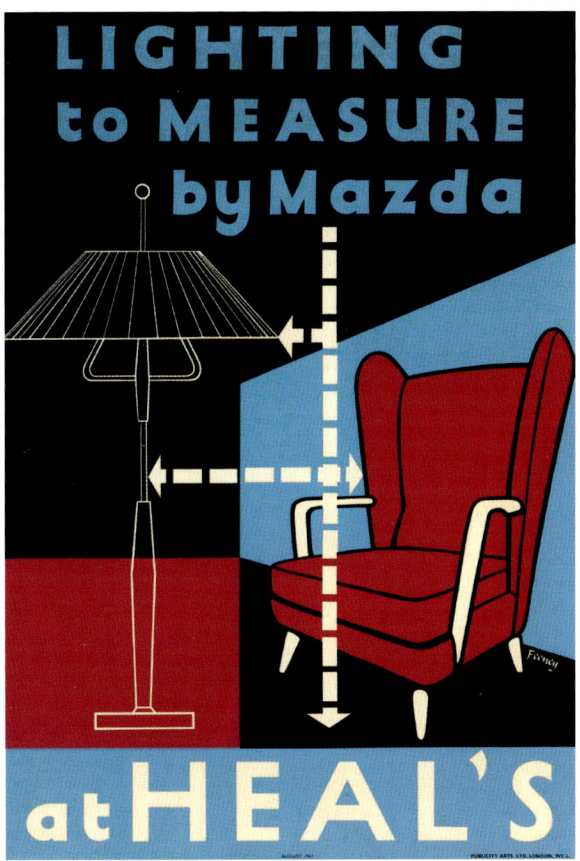

Opposite page: Christmas window display at Heal's, 1965.

Above: Promotional marketing for 'Christmas Eve at Heal's', 1965.

Right: Heal's poster focusing on childrens gifts, 1960s.

# Epilogue

Heal's posters, inviting potential customers to visit, reflected the history of the shop itself, through good times and challenging times, the ups and downs of an enterprise with its periods of confidence and confusion.

Their images chartered the fashions, the trends, of British twentieth century furniture design as it moved from Arts and Crafts and oak, to bentwood and chrome, to metal and plastics, from the early tentative essays into modernism in the 1920s through to its lingering days in the post-war years.

Opposite page: 'Head over Heal's', billboard publicity from more recent times, 1999.

Right: Early publicity design, 'Heal's for Beds – British', 1926.

By their overall design Heal's posters, their typography and images and the interplay of the two, mirrored the development of twentieth century graphics, leaving behind Victorian heavy ornamentation, plunging into modernist reductionism, through to a simplified lightheartedness.

And, as Heal's led the field in furniture and furnishing design, whether its own, commissioned or imported, yet none of it excessive or radical, so Heal's posters had a kind of restraint, even politeness to them. If they had energy and impact it lay somewhere between the 'force' implied by Timmers definition of a poster and Ambrose's 'pleasant' – interesting and oftimes intriguing, without being demanding. If Heal's was on a mission to educate and enlighten as well as to sell, its posters served it well.

# Bibliography

1935   Harry Trethowan, *Selling through the window*, The Studio Limited.

1972   *Heal's Catalogues 1853–1934*, Heal & Sons.

1972   Sir Ambrose Heal, *A booklet to commemorate the Centenary exhibition of the life and work of Sir Ambrose Heal*, Heal's.

1984   Susanna Gooden, *At the Sign of the Fourposter*, Heal & Son.

2004   Peyton Skipworth, *Britain between the wars 1918–1939*, Fine Art Society.

2006   Deborah Cohen, *Household Gods: The British and their possessions*, Yale University Press.

2013   Ruth Artmonsky, *Showing Off: Fifty years of London store publicity and display*, Artmonsky Arts.

2013   Lesley Jackson, *Modern British Furniture Design since 1945*, V&A.

2014   Oliver S. Heal, *Sir Ambrose Heal and the Heal Cabinet Factory 1897–1939*, Oblong.

2016   Ruth Artmonsky, *Tuppence Plain, Penny Coloured: Fifty years of furniture advertising and selling*, Artmonsky Arts.

# Appendix
## Artists producing posters at Heal's 1917–1980

**Bernard Adeney (1878–1966)**
b. London; Studied at Royal Academy Schools, Academie Julian in Paris, the Slade. Founder member of the London Group (its President 1921–3). Taught textiles at Central School from 1903 (Head of Department 1930–47). WWII worked in camouflage for Tank Corps. Official war artist. Designed textiles for Liberty's, Allan Walton Textiles.

**Maxwell Armfield (1881–1972)**
b. Hampshire; studied at Birmingham School of Art, Paris, Italy, United States (1915–22). Settled in Cotswolds. Designed textiles, illustrated c. 20 books, wrote books on painting, exhibited R.A., NEAC, Leicester Galleries.

**Sydney Samuel Arrobus (1901–1990)**
b. London; known as a Hampstead artist. Studied at Heatherley's School of Fine Art. Showed at London art clubs and venues around Hampstead. WWII served with Field Security Section and Psychological Warfare Branch in Europe and in the Middle East, sketching his experiences.

**Keith Baynes (1887–1977)**
b. Reigate, Surrey; studied at Cambridge and the Slade (1912–15). Member of Friday Club, London Group, London Artist's Association. oil painter exhibited widely in U.K. and overseas in galleries incl. Ashmolean and Fitzwilliam. Retrospective at The Minories, Colchester, 1969.

**Ernest John Biggs (1896–1986)**
b. Otley, Yorkshire; worked in an architect's office. Studied at Birmingham School of Art; worked for printers; WWI served in France (lost leg); worked in advertising dept. of Kendrick & Jefferson, West Bromich printers until 1923; moved to London; worked at Crawford's advertising agency; early 1920s worked at London Press Exchange; worked in advertising in Netherlands and Sweden; worked for Erwin Wasey; art director London Press Exchange; WWII anti-nazi propaganda unit in Scandinavia. Wrote *Colour in Advertising*, 1956. Work in British Museum.

**Vernon Blake (1875–1930)**
b. Reigate; author, journalist, sculptor, painter, inventor; studied art Paris and Florence; Director of the British School at Rome; designed war memorials; wrote for art and design magazines. Wrote *Relation in Art*, 1925.

**Frank Brangwyn (1867–1956)**
b. Bruges, Belgium; largely self-taught; painter and designer of stained glass, textiles, furniture, ceramics; produced over 12,000 works; WWI posters and lithographs; work in British Museum, William Morris Gallery and in Bruges; Royal Academician; knighted 1941.

**Betty Hilda Cooke (1907–1982)**
b. Edinburgh; studied Ruskin School of Drawing and Fine Art; worked as graphic designer (incl. posters for Southern Railway); designed textiles for Edinburgh Weavers and Sanderson's. Work in V&A.

### Alan Cracknell (b. 1937)
b. Harrow Illustrator of books, publicity, advertisements e.g. for Orient Express, Crabtree & Evelyn. Work in British Council Collection.

### Rhoda Dawson (1897–1992)
b. London; studied Hammersmith School of Art; worked at Heal's until 1930; taught crafts with Grenfell Medical Mission in Canada; studied archaeology and worked for Gunnersby Museum.

### Marguerite Dorlng (1894–1977)
b. London; exhibited R.A. and Grosvenor Galleries 1920s/30s; posters for London Underground in 1920s. Work in V&A and London Transport Museum.

### Sheila Dunn (fl. 1920–1957)
Studied at St. John's Wood School of Art; fashion illustration for *Vogue*; cartoons for *Punch*; graphics for Lotus and Delta Shoes, Cadbury's and Morley's Silk Stockings; illustrated children's books.

### Charles Feeney (fl. 1950–1960s)
Brought up in Malta; attained National Diploma in Design and Associateship of the Institute of British Decorators; worked in interior decoration; joined Heal's in 1950; display for Heal's as well as prolific poster designer 1950s/60s. Retired to Spain.

### Alan Fletcher (1931–2006)
b. Nairobi; four art schools: Hammersmith, Central, RCA, Yale. Major graphic designer; founded design studio with Colin Forbes and Bob Gill; partnership evolved into Pentagram 1971; des. logos incl. V&A, IoD; art director Phaidon Press; retrospective Design Museum 2006; wrote, incl. *The Art of Looking Sideways*.

### Claud Lovat Fraser (1890–1921)
b. London; worked in solicitor's; largely self-taught (6 months at Westminster School of Art under Sickert); stage designer; designed toys and textiles; WWI War Office; graphic designs for Curwen Press; advertising graphics; book illustration.

### Percy Robert Gossop (1876–1951)
b. London; apprentice wallpaper and fabric dsigner; studied part-time Birkbeck College and Hammersmith School of Art; freelance designer and illustrator (1896–1902); studio manager

Eyre & Spottiswood, printers (1902–4); W.H. Smith's studio; first art editor British Vogue; art adviser to Edinburgh printers; WWI Ministry of Information; 1918 joint manager Carlton Studios; own artists agency; co-founded S.I.A with Milner Gray; lecturer City of London College; wrote *Advertising Design*, 1927; archive in V&A.

## Arthur Greenwood (c. 1900–1990)
Trained at Shoreditch Technical Institute; joined Heal's 1916 – his whole career was with Heal's; converted Ambrose's sketches into working drawings; considered father of the Drawing Office.

## F.H.K. Henrion (1914–1990)
b. Nuremburg, Germany; to Paris 1933 worked in textile studio; attended Ecole Paul Colin, training as poster designer; 1936 to London; WWII at Ministry of Information; set up own studio 1948; leading figure in corporate identity design; taught at art schools – Head of Visual Communication, London College of Printing; active in professional bodies internationally.

## Frederick Charles Herrick (1887–1970)
b. Barrow-in-Furness; studied at Leicester College of Arts & Crafts and R.C.A; after WWI joined Baynard Press becoming Head of Studio; designed lion logo for the British Empire Exhibition 1924; produced 45 posters for London Underground (1920–1934); posters for railway and shipping companies; 1930s taught at Sir John Cass School of Art and then, for decades, Brighton School of Art.

## Hilaire Hiler (1898–1966)
b. Minnesota, U.S.; attended Rhode Island School of Design and Pennsylvania schools of Fine Art and of Industrial Art; worked in U.S. and Europe; lived in Paris 1919–1934; showed in Leicester Galleries 1926–1932); 1934 returned to U.S.; muralist, theatre designer, teacher, author, colour theorist.

## Rodney Hooper (b. 1911 fl. 1930s–50s)
Furniture designer/maker; author – Modern Furniture making and Design, 1939; *Woodcraft in Design and Practice*, 1947; *Plastics for the Home Craftsman*, 1953.

### Edward McKnight Kauffer (1890–1954)
b. Montana, U.S.; worked as scene painter for publisher and bookseller whilst attending evening classes at Mark Hopkins Institute; studied short for periods at Chicago Art Institute; came to Paris 1913, and then London; became London Underground's most prolific poster designer; exhibited with London Group and Group X; most progressive and influential graphic designer in U.K. in inter-war years; returned to U.S. 1939.

### Nicholas de Molas (1900–1944)
b. St. Petersburg, Russia; studied painting Moscow and Prague; studied theatre design Marinsky Theatre School, Petrograd; moved to U.K.; painter/sculptor; photographer and designer for textiles, fashion and theatre; painted murals and ceilings in U.K., Paris and U.S.; designed fabrics and wallpapers for Fortnum & Mason.

### Paul Nash (1889–1946)
b. London; attended Bolt Court (LCC) and Slade (left early); showed at London Galleries from 1912; WWI official war artist; taught in Oxford and at R.C.A from 1924; worked as artist and designer(textiles, glass, ceramics, theatre); wrote books and articles on art; member of Unit One Group; WWII attached to Air Ministry; notable for war paintings.

### Herry (Heather) Perry (1897–1962)
b. Bolton; trained Central School of Arts & Crafts; prolific poster designer for London Underground – over 50; specialist designer of illustrated maps for posters, advertising and murals e.g. Queen Mary.

### James Porter (1883–1944)
b. New Zealand; studied Academie Julian, Paris; from c 1916 showed with London Group (1925–35 Vice-President); founder member London Artists' Association; showed at London Galleries; taught at Central School of Arts & Crafts (1924–44); work in Tate and provincial galleries.

### William Roberts (1895–1980)
b. London; apprentice to poster firm, Joseph Causton & Sons Ltd.; evening classes St. Martins; studied at Slade (1910–1913); exhibited Group X, the London Group, London Artists' Association; exhibited R.A. – elected 1966; wrote pamphlets; a

number of retrospective exhibitions – Arts Council at Tate 1965, Reading 1983, N.P.G. 1984, Ben Uri 2003, Reading 1983; taught at Central School of Arts & Crafts; work in Tate and numerous provincial galleries.

### Norman Weaver (1913–1989)
b. London; attended Hammersmith School of Art; joined Heal's in Cabinet Making Department before becoming its manuscript writer and calligrapher for some five years, attended art evening classes and then Central; began teaching there up to 1939; WWII Ordinance Survey/ Royal Engineers; joined Beverley Pick exhibition design; 1952 Artists' Partners Ltd advertisement design incl. Wilkinson's Swords logo; designed postage stamps; illustrated nature books; wrote book on drawing insects; retired to Isle of Wight.

### Pamela F.F. Wrightson (married name Barnett) (1927–1971)
b. Islington; attended Hampstead Garden Suburb Institute for calligraphy; worked at Heal's 1947–1966; calligrapher for non-Heal's commissions; designed exhibition posters for Society of Scribes & Illuminators; served on Society's committee in 1960s; work in V&A.

*Other artists providing Heal's posters incl. Miss Bowden, Geoffrey Dunn, Ann Fisher, Greiwerth, Paul Henry, Ann Philipson, Helen Senior, S.A. Watkins.*